the HOMEMADE
vegan
pantry

the HOMEMADE
vegan
pantry

the ART of MAKING
YOUR OWN STAPLES

MIYOKO SCHINNER

PHOTOGRAPHY BY EVA KOLENKO

TEN SPEED PRESS
Berkeley

contents

foreword

I am a fan of cookbooks. I write them myself, but more important, I read them. I guess you could even say I breathe cookbooks. Not a wall in my home is without an overflowing bookcase full of them. Some are pristine and untouched, some are loaded with sticky notes, and some are a little too manhandled by sticky fingers. A few of those are written by Miyoko.

And so, I hope it doesn't seem odd that a cookbook author is writing a foreword for another cookbook. You'd think that we'd all be gently elbowing each other out of the way for shelf space, but that is exactly why I wanted to write this in the first place.

Vegan cooking has a larger mission than, say, molecular gastronomy or French cuisine. As important as those cuisines are—to our taste buds and culturally, too—they don't have the same sense of urgency. Because vegan cooking is, well, not to sound overly dramatic, trying to save the world.

Sometimes we forget about the other stuff, and the saving-the-world part takes precedent.

Now, I'm not about to come down on anyone for choosing to give up animal products and reaching for the nearest meat analogue on the supermarket shelves. I'm happy that those things exist! However, I'd argue that the taste bud and cultural parts of vegan cooking are just as important, and in fact, we can't save the world unless we make those connections.

We need to go beyond vegan cooking. We need vegan cuisine.

Luckily, we've got the entire plant kingdom at our disposal. Vegan cuisine is uniquely positioned to be the next wave of cooking, because we can pull from every other culture and continent. Every single herb and spice, for instance, is vegan. It might seem a silly thing to say, but it comes in handy to remember when so often we're told that vegan food is limiting.

But not only do herbivores need to love the food, so does everyone else, too. And, if I can get a bit brazen, I'd say: it doesn't really matter if vegans love it. What matters is that everyone else does.

And that's where Miyoko comes in.

The first time I saw her was at a vegan event in Portland (of course), looking badass in a skirt and heels I could never pull off. She was certainly a commanding figure with that alone. But she also happened to be holding a big tray of vegan cheese. And I don't mean "cheeze" with a z. I'm talking cheese! It was cultured and aged and nuanced and complex and creamy and rindy and stinky and eyes-roll-to-the-back-of-your-head delicious.

Really, one bite and I knew, it's the only thing that will save the world. Because if everyone could eat like that, everyone would. And thankfully, Miyoko is sharing all of her mouthwatering recipes right here in this book.

The Homemade Vegan Pantry makes world-class vegan dishes possible for everyone at every skill level. This is all thanks to Miyoko, a chef who not only makes the best vegan cheese ever but also brings a passion to her recipes that gets both herbivores and omnivores excited about quality food that isn't as hard to make as the average person might think.

Miyoko is right there on the front lines, pushing vegan cuisine forward. Where other chefs throw down their whisks in exhaustion as they attempt to perfect vegan meringue (okay, well, I'm talking about myself here), Miyoko is there, whisking away until she achieves light, fluffy perfection.

Let's follow her there, mixing bowls in hand!

From Omaha,
Isa Chandra Moskowitz

introduction

Like many of you, I'm a busy parent with a busy career. Let's be honest—as a chef, I love creating new dishes, inventing food products, or preparing fancy meals for dinner parties. But it can become a chore to put dinner on the table every night. It can be a chore just to think about what to put on the table every night. So, like most people, as my family grew and life became more complicated, I began to buy more packaged and premade goods, primarily things we consider to be staples, like vegan mayonnaise, marinara, veggie burgers, and so on, but sometimes even frozen entrées, like pizza and veggie chicken. While all of this seemed to make my life easier, Mother Nature wasn't smiling down on me on garbage night as our family's mountain of packaging waste grew, nor did it help our pocketbook, our health, or our enjoyment of the taste and flavors of food.

What if I just stopped buying many commercial products and started making them myself? I shook with fear—the thought alone was exhausting. I knew that homemade versions of many of these staples were superior in flavor and worth the sacrifice of a bit of time—if I had the time. After all, I like "slow food"—but I just want it fast.

But as I thought about it, I realized that over all my years of cooking, I'd stumbled upon a number of shortcuts for classic dishes. Mind you, I can't take credit for all of the tricks, but there are a number of methods for making things faster and easier. It turns out some "sacred steps" aren't really sacred or critical at all. You don't have to stand at the stove all day stirring risotto or polenta, for example—you can just stir once and then throw it in your oven and let it do the rest. As famed New York baker Jim Lahey and others have shown, there's no need to knead, a revelation that reduces bread-making to a 2-minute proposition. Making a pound of delicious, creamy vegan butter takes 90 seconds, which is probably less time than it takes to make the trek from the produce section to the butter section of your grocer. And a 60-second raw marinara that is frozen becomes a lovely cooked sauce when thawed and heated briefly.

So I started bypassing the freezer section. And one day, I made soy yogurt for the first time in years and remembered how easy it was. And then I made mayo. Then bread. Then butter to put on the bread. And eventually, the soy milk to wash it all down. And in between, so many of the other staples that fill this book, as well as the dishes that use the homemade staples. And somehow, I still had time to make those nightly dinners, and they got better because of my pantry of homemade goods.

I found that taking just a few minutes to fill your larder with staples pays off in the end, saving you hours. Take the baking mixes, for example. So you spend 10 minutes to create a multiuse mix. When you need cookies for the potluck or muffins for breakfast, you can capture that "baked from scratch" flavor in just moments. On a leisurely Sunday, make a large batch of UnSteak (page 127) so you can grab it from your freezer for a quick meal during the week. And all the classics—mayonnaise, ketchup, mustard, butter—take but a few minutes to whip up but will add panache to your cooking for weeks.

I also developed ways to create multiple products from one recipe and reduce food waste. For example, why go to the trouble to cook up a beautiful pot of stock from scratch, then toss out the veggies? Why not turn those spent veggies into something else? In this book, I give you bonus recipes for turning them into pâté (see page 87), soup (see page 82), and even veggie dogs (page 120). Or roasted tomatoes (page 33), which are marvelous, but the by-products of which are even more amazing. Who would think that the usually discarded, lowly skins could become a zesty pesto for soups and sandwiches (page 36), or that their run-off juices could add so much to risottos (page 35) and polenta? How about homemade vanilla extract (page 203) that makes use of that bottle of vodka left over from a party and leaves you with fragrant vanilla pods that in turn become vanilla paste, leaving nothing to waste? A single food or dish has many lives.

Getting into the kitchen and building your own pantry has other benefits besides convenience. Did I mention you'd save money? Quite a bit, in fact. Consider that half gallon of soy milk that costs around four dollars at the store. To make the same amount at home takes a couple of handfuls of soybeans (maybe fifty cents) and some water. How about some of that high-end vegan aioli-style mayonnaise? Another four bucks. But use some oil, homemade soy milk, a little garlic, and some seasonings, and you've got yourself some fancy spread for sandwiches at a fraction of the cost. So what are the savings? Not 20 percent, not 30 percent, not even 40 percent. On many items, you'll save up to 80 percent compared to buying the commercially made equivalent.

And what about health benefits? When everything is made at home, you'll know and be able to control what goes into your food, unlike store-bought products with their mysterious, unpronounceable ingredients. I've provided leeway in many recipes that allows you to be as pure and clean—or as indulgent—as you want. This isn't a health book, but there are plenty of healthful options presented. Although I eat, and advocate eating, as unprocessed and clean a diet as possible, with minimal or no use of oil or sugar, I find that for some dishes, nothing else suffices. But if you're looking for an everyday mayonnaise or a great granola, you'll find completely oil- and sugar-free versions in here. I'll let you decide how pure you want to be, and I provide you recipes that let you decide whether to go rich or lean.

Then there's the environment. You probably recycle, shop at farmers' markets, buy local as much as you can, use public transportation, and maybe even put solar on your house. If you're vegan or vegetarian, you most likely already know the heavy impact of livestock production on the global environment and how eating low on the food chain—that is, a plant-based diet—can minimize those impacts. If you're vegan, you're already doing your part to save energy, water, resources, and land use—up to 90 percent over omnivores, according to some studies. So what am I talking about? Buying prepackaged goods means producing a heck of a lot more waste—soy milk containers, jars, bottles, plastic tubs, other packaging— some of it recyclable, some of it not. But even the recycling process uses energy and resources, not to mention the energy that goes into producing the packaging in the first place.

If you're concerned about the environment and are not already a full-time vegan, using this book will have an even greater impact on the planet. According to studies conducted by the United Nations,[1] the World Bank,[2] and numerous other organizations, the single biggest contributor to greenhouse gases isn't your SUV, but livestock production. Up to 51 percent of all greenhouse gases—and many of them far more potent than CO_2 in raising the Earth's temperature—are a direct result of producing animals for human consumption. This is far more than all global transportation put together. In a nutshell, we grow crops to feed animals to feed ourselves. We're talking 80 to 90 percent of all soybeans, wheat, and corn grown worldwide are feed for livestock. Imagine the massive amount of water, energy, and land that takes (over 30 percent of all global land mass). It's mind-boggling. What if we just ate the crops ourselves? Just reflect on the savings in land, water, energy, resources, pollution—and animals' lives. So even if you can't afford to buy a Prius, you can, in fact, decrease your global footprint dramatically by going vegan. It is empowering to know that each and every one of us can actually do something to affect what is seemingly so overwhelming, simply by changing what's on our plates.

Finally, there's flavor. Twenty-five years ago, when I wrote my first cookbook, *The Now and Zen Epicure* (Book Publishing Company, 1991), I stressed that I wanted to entice people to a plant-based diet not through ideology but through their taste buds. I still hold that philosophy close to my heart—let the aromas wafting from my kitchen lure you within! And when you taste, you shall believe. In other words, I write not just for vegans and vegetarians, but also for anyone interested in delicious, homemade food, and I hope that by creating such, I can make it easier to adopt a vegan diet. When you can make delicious, carefully crafted food without harming animals, the planet, or your health, it's a win-win for everybody. And that's why, in my book, it's the most beautiful food.

This book isn't just about the staples themselves. It's about how they set the rhythm for adopting a time-honored, handcrafted approach to cooking in general. It's about slowing down enough to imagine, even if only very occasionally, that as you stand at your kitchen counter, you are really in Tuscany preparing a meal to be enjoyed under an arbor heavy with grapes—maybe some hand-thrown pasta with a simple, rustic sauce, a caprese salad, and a carafe of refreshing wine. Immersed in our hectic lives, it seems but a wistful thought to hearken back to an age or place when and where we might enjoy things made slowly with care, in small batches, in an artisanal way. If only we could! And I say, we can!

It's about more than food. It's about a mind-set that lets you slow down enough to care about what is truly meaningful: the luscious joy of creating simple but beautiful things, things that sing in your mouth with their purity and honesty, and then sharing them with others. Unprocessed, uncomplicated, unabashed. And it's all done in your kitchen. Your artisanal kitchen, created from the bottom up. It all starts with building a rock-solid foundation, a foundation of staples that enhance every morsel of food that comes out of there.

So now, step into my kitchen and join me in reinventing and re-creating our pantries.

---

1 Food and Agricultural Organization of the United Nations, *Livestock's Long Shadow: Environmental Issues and Options*, 2006, www.fao.org/docrep/010/a0701e/a0701e00.HTM.

2 Robert Goodland and Jeff Anhang, "Livestock and Climate Change: What If the Key Actors in Climate Change Are . . . Cows, Pigs, and Chickens?," *World Watch Magazine* 22 (no. 6), November/December 2009, www.worldwatch.org/files/pdf/Livestock%20and%20Climate%20Change.pdf.

condiments

What would life be without our condiments to bring zest to our food? All substance and no style, that's what. And that would be no fun. (If you've ever tried cooking while on the road, you know what I'm talking about.) A good ketchup can make or break a burger, and a fragrant jam can transport you and your humble piece of toast to the cafés of Paris. And then there are the flavor enhancers that many of us vegans thought we had to kiss good-bye, like Worcestershire or fish sauce. Well, hello again!

It might seem daunting to go as far as making your own mustard. But I invite you to get down and dirty in your kitchen to inject artistry into your pantry. Is it hard? Or labor-intensive? If it were, I wouldn't bother! With a few tweaks, most of the recipes here have been streamlined so that they whip up in just minutes (or seconds) but provide weeks of enjoyment. So don't hold back—get started and bring some zing to all of your dishes!

classic eggless mayonnaise

With a marvelous rich flavor and thick, creamy texture, this will easily become your go-to mayo for everything from sandwiches to potato salad.

1 cup soy milk or other nondairy milk

1 to 2 tablespoons mustard

1 tablespoon apple cider vinegar or freshly squeezed lemon juice

1 teaspoon sea salt or black salt (kala namak; see sidebar)

1 teaspoon organic sugar (optional)

1½ to 2½ cups canola or other neutral oil

Place the soy milk, mustard, vinegar, salt, and sugar (if you like your mayonnaise sweeter, like Miracle Whip) in a blender and process briefly. With the blender running, add the oil in a very thin, steady stream (and I mean a *very* thin stream) until it turns very thick and the blender has trouble processing (if you have a high- or multispeed blender, use a medium speed). Thickening will not happen gradually, but rather suddenly, and may take as long as 4 minutes altogether. Also, please note that the amount of oil necessary for thickening will depend on the speed of your blender and how slowly you pour, and can vary by as much as a cup. Transfer to a jar and store in the refrigerator for up to 1 month.

MAKES 3 TO 3½ CUPS

BLACK SALT

Black salt, or kala namak, a highly sulfuric-smelling and -tasting salt from India, is actually pinkish in color. It lends an egglike flavor to dishes. It can be ordered online or found at some Indian grocers.

VARIATION

AIOLI Add 4 to 6 cloves of garlic to the soy milk. Substitute lemon juice for the vinegar and extra-virgin olive oil for the canola oil.

lemon cashew mayo

If you're looking for a soy-free mayonnaise, try this. It's light, refreshing, and perky, just perfect for cucumber sandwiches!

½ cup cashews

½ cup water

3 tablespoons freshly squeezed lemon juice

1 teaspoon sea salt

1½ to 2 cups canola or olive oil or a mixture

½ teaspoon xanthan gum (optional)

Place the cashews, water, lemon juice, and salt in a blender and puree until smooth. If the mixture feels warm, let it cool to room temperature before proceeding. With the blender running, pour in the oil in a slow, steady, very thin stream until very thick; this may take 3 to 4 minutes. If the mixture does not seem quite as thick as regular mayonnaise, rest assured that it will thicken to a spreadable consistency in the refrigerator. If you want it really stiff, blend in the xanthan gum, then pour the mayonnaise into a jar and store in the refrigerator for up to 1 month.

MAKES ABOUT 2½ CUPS

oil-free eggless mayo

If you are trying to minimize your use of oil (as I do, except when a culinary application simply requires it), then this spread fits the bill. It works not only in sandwiches but also as a foundation for any mayonnaise-based sauce. I serve this all the time, and people don't notice that it's oil-free. If you can save 100 calories a tablespoon, why not?

½ cup cashews, soaked for 3 to 4 hours and drained

½ cup water

12 ounces medium, regular, or medium-firm tofu (don't use extra firm or vacuum-packed)

2 tablespoons apple cider vinegar

2 teaspoons mustard

1 teaspoon maple syrup, organic sugar, or agave

1 teaspoon sea salt

½ teaspoon xanthan gum

Puree the cashews and water in a blender until smooth. Add the tofu, vinegar, mustard, maple syrup, and sea salt and process until creamy. Finally, add the xanthan gum and process again for a few seconds. It will continue to thicken in the refrigerator. This keeps for about 3 weeks in the fridge.

MAKES ABOUT 2 CUPS

squeeze bottle yellow mustard

This is the traditional stuff that goes on everything. It gets cooked, which mellows it out, so you can use it right away, unlike the "fancy pants" mustards that follow.

¾ cup powdered mustard

¾ cup distilled white vinegar

½ cup water

1 teaspoon turmeric

1 teaspoon sea salt

½ teaspoon garlic powder

½ teaspoon paprika

1 teaspoon cornstarch or arrowroot

In a medium bowl, whisk together all of the ingredients, or add everything to a blender and mix until smooth. Pour the mixture into a saucepan and simmer over low heat for 8 to 10 minutes, stirring frequently. Pour the mustard into a jar or squeeze bottle. It will thicken as it cools. Keep your mustard in a squeeze bottle or jar in the refrigerator for many months or in your pantry for up to 2 or 3 months.

MAKES ABOUT 1½ CUPS

dijon mustard

The two most frequently found mustard seeds are white and brown.
White is mellower; brown is zingier. (So-called yellow mustard is made
with white mustard seeds with turmeric added to it.) I make most of
my mustards with brown seeds, but white have a place in my heart, too.
I buy my mustard seeds online or at Indian grocery stores, where they
are very cheap. Of course, you can use powdered mustard, but I prefer to
use the seeds, which can be pureed to be very smooth or left with some
texture for character. There's only one caveat: you'll have to wait a couple
of weeks or more to taste your 1-minute culinary effort, or it might just
go right up your nose, like when you put too much wasabi on your sushi.
Mustard needs time to mellow, but once it's made, it lasts almost forever.

½ cup brown mustard seeds

½ cup white wine

¼ cup apple cider vinegar

¼ cup water

1 teaspoon sea salt

Combine all of the ingredients in a jar. Let it macerate for 1 to 2 days. Place in a
blender and puree until it is as smooth as you like. Pack it in a jar and store at room
temperature for 2 to 4 weeks to mellow. When it's mellowed to your liking, move
it to the fridge, where it will keep for 1 year.

MAKES 1½ CUPS

ale and brown sugar mustard

With a hint of caramel sweetness and bitter notes from the ale, this complex mustard will elevate your burgers, hot dogs, and sausages.

½ cup brown mustard seeds

½ cup ale

½ cup water

¼ cup apple cider vinegar

2 to 3 tablespoons brown sugar or coconut sugar

1 teaspoon sea salt

Combine all of the ingredients in a jar. You can use more or less sugar depending on the sweetness desired (both brown sugar and coconut sugar add a caramel note, but brown sugar is sweeter). Let it macerate for 1 or 2 days. Place in a blender and puree until it is as smooth as you like. Pack it in a jar and store at room temperature for 2 to 4 weeks until it's mellowed to your liking. Then move it to the fridge, where it will keep for 1 year.

MAKES 1¾ CUPS

CUSTOMIZE YOUR MUSTARD

All those little jars of expensive mustards can be yours for the making in just a few short minutes. The variations are endless—try sweet honey (vegan honey, of course!) mustard or orange ginger mustard or get creative—with mustard, anything goes.

Mustard is basically mustard powder or seeds mixed with a liquid.

The general rules for mustard making are these:

1. Use a 2:1 or 2½:1 ratio of liquid to seeds. Be creative with the liquid used; plain water is fine, but how about wine, beer, vinegar, juice, or kombucha? Using flavors such as citrus zest, sweeteners, herbs, and spices will add character. As the mixture sits, it will thicken.

2. To expedite the mellowing process and make for easier grinding, soak the seeds in the liquids and seasonings for a couple of days.

3. Toss it all in a blender and puree until it's as smooth as you like.

4. Pack it into jars and store at room temperature for 2 to 3 weeks, until it mellows. Refrigeration stops the mellowing process and it will stay forever zingy, so don't chill it until it's ready! Then make a great sandwich.

basic ketchup

In 1994, the night before I opened my first vegan restaurant, Now and Zen Bistro, in San Francisco, I realized we had a burger on the menu but no actual recipe. Happily, I met with success that night when I created the Now and Zen Burger (page 133, renamed The Real UnBurger). But when you have a burger, you also have to have ketchup. Back in the day, the only ketchup options were the nonorganic varieties filled with corn syrup, which certainly couldn't grace our tables. So I quickly whipped some up. The next day, we had burgers, and we had ketchup.

So what is ketchup? It's basically tomato paste with vinegar, a sweetener, and some salt. It is so ridiculously easy to make that once you learn how, it will boggle your mind that you ever spent any money buying it.

2 (6-ounce) cans tomato paste (1⅓ cups)

⅔ cup water

⅓ cup apple cider vinegar

¼ cup organic sugar

2 teaspoons sea salt

Place all of the ingredients in a medium bowl, and stir until the sugar is dissolved. This can also be done in a food processor. Store it in a jar in the fridge, where it'll keep for a couple of months.

MAKES ABOUT 2 CUPS

VARIATIONS

MAPLE BALSAMIC KETCHUP Substitute maple syrup for the sugar, and balsamic vinegar for the apple cider vinegar.

SMOKY KETCHUP To the Basic Ketchup, add 1 teaspoon or more of smoked paprika.

SPANISH KETCHUP Substitute red or white wine vinegar for the apple cider vinegar, add 1 teaspoon of garlic and 1 teaspoon of onion powder, then chop up some olives and throw them into the mix.

SPICY MEXICAN KETCHUP To the Basic Ketchup, add 1 finely chopped chipotle pepper in adobo sauce, $\frac{1}{2}$ teaspoon of garlic powder, and 1 teaspoon of ground cumin.

CUSTOMIZE YOUR KETCHUP

Making ketchup yourself opens it up to infinite variations in flavor by using different kinds of vinegars, sweeteners, and even salts. You can even infuse it with flavors like smoked paprika or chipotle peppers to add other dimensions. It takes but moments to prepare, and you only have to follow these four simple rules:

1. Use tomato paste.

2. Use some type of vinegar—experiment! Try balsamic vinegar, wine vinegar, rice vinegar, sherry vinegar, or even fancy fruit-flavored vinegars.

3. Use some type of sweetener—sugar, agave, maple syrup, coconut sugar, even pureed dates.

4. Use salt of some type, such as smoked or flavored ones, but make sure it's not coarse or it may not dissolve.

That's it! Stir it up and then make some fries.

erster (oyster) sauce

I have a confession. For years after I became a vegetarian as a preteen, I didn't make the connection between oyster sauce and oysters. I don't know why, but I just thought it was some brown sauce, the origins of which I didn't think to reflect on (or maybe because veggies with oyster sauce are often under the "vegetarian" section of Chinese restaurants). So perhaps that disqualifies me from having been a true vegetarian in those early years. Then one day, while eating some Chinese veggies with oyster sauce, I offered some to another vegetarian friend, who declined, having done a bit more research than I had. Sometimes we can be really naïve.

Since then, I've used commercial vegetarian oyster sauce available at Asian markets, but I generally find them only sweet and salty, lacking the umami that oyster sauce lends. So I developed this, which gets its complexity from shiitakes and nori. It's not as deeply brown as the kind containing real oysters, but hey, as the old Gershwin tune goes, I say erster.

1 cup hot water

4 or 5 dried shiitakes

¼ cup soy sauce or tamari

2 tablespoons organic sugar or agave

1 sheet nori, folded and torn into little pieces

4 teaspoons cornstarch

Pour the hot water over the mushrooms in a small bowl. Let them soak for 1 hour, or until completely soft throughout. If you're not sure, slice one down the middle and see if it is tender. Put the mushrooms and soaking liquid into a blender along with the other ingredients and process until thick, smooth, and creamy. Transfer the mixture to a small saucepan and cook for a few minutes over medium heat until hot and thickened. Store in a jar in the refrigerator for up to 1 month.

MAKES 1¼ CUPS

"I say oyster, and you say erster . . ."
—George Gershwin

teriyaki sauce

Being Japanese, I don't put teriyaki sauce into the exotic, ethnic cuisine category. It's what I throw together to flavor veggies, tofu, seitan, or whatever I'm cooking when I'm too tired to think creatively. But I don't tire of it; it's an old friend that'll probably be with me as long as I can stand at the stove. Here's an easy version you'll reach for time and time again.

¼ cup sesame seeds

½ cup soy sauce

½ cup mirin (sweet sake; see sidebar)

⅓ cup organic sugar, coconut sugar, or brown rice syrup

1¼ cups water

1 tablespoon arrowroot or cornstarch

Put the sesame seeds in a dry skillet and toast over low heat for 2 to 3 minutes, until they start to pop. Be careful—they can burn fast, so remove them from the heat when they start to pop and their aroma fills the room.

Combine the soy sauce, mirin, sugar, and water in a saucepan and bring to a simmer over medium heat for 3 or 4 minutes. Dissolve the arrowroot in a tablespoon or two of water, and whisk into the sauce to thicken. Stir in the sesame seeds. Store in a jar in your pantry or fridge for several weeks, if it lasts that long.

MAKES ABOUT 2 CUPS

MIRIN

Mirin is a sweet sake that rounds out flavors and adds depth. It's generally available at better grocery, natural food, and Asian stores. Try to find naturally brewed mirin, which will not contain corn syrup or other sweeteners. It should have only rice and koji, an enzyme used for making sake, miso, and vinegars.

vegan fish sauce

When I dine at Vietnamese and Thai restaurants and request that they leave out the fish sauce, ubiquitous in South Asian cuisine, the dishes sometimes taste as if they are lacking something. That "something" is fish sauce, South Asia's "secret ingredient" that adds oomph to dishes, injecting that special flavor that you can't quite put your finger on. Here is my vegan version that can be universally added to Asian-style dishes, lending them that extra "something." And the secret ingredients in my fish sauce? Wakame, a seaweed, and the liquid from those jars of fermented tofu, a somewhat stinky Chinese condiment made by preserving tofu in wine, vinegar, and other ingredients for months (don't be put off by the description!). Give it a try and then use it in everything from green papaya salad to Thai-style curries.

¾ cup water

2 tablespoons organic sugar

2 tablespoons soy sauce or Bragg's Liquid Aminos

1 tablespoon distilled vinegar

2 tablespoons liquid from a jar of fermented tofu (see sidebar)

1 teaspoon Wakame Powder (recipe follows)

1 teaspoon sea salt

Combine all of the ingredients in a jar and mix or shake well. Store in the refrigerator for up to 2 months. Shake well each time before using to redistribute the wakame.

MAKES ABOUT 1 CUP

FERMENTED TOFU

Fermented tofu is a type of preserved tofu that is brined in salt, water, and wine. It is quite pungent in flavor and smell, and has a creamy consistency. It is sold in little jars in Asian grocery stores.

wakame powder

I thought I'd share my little secret for adding the flavor of the ocean to dishes. It's wakame, a type of seaweed that is frequently sold broken up in pieces in little bags.

I like to pulverize it in a blender until it's reduced to a fine green powder. Sprinkled into soups and sauces, it'll make just about anything taste mildly, well, fishy (kelp powder can work, too, but it's not as flavorful). It's also delicious mixed into rice and other grains, where it amplifies the nutritional content, boosting iodine, calcium, protein, and micronutrients multifold. You'll find it used in several recipes in this book, and I hope you'll try sprinkling it on salads, soups, grains, and other dishes to add flavor and nutrients.

1 cup dried wakame

Put the wakame in a blender and cover tightly. Process until it is completely pulverized. Wait a second for the wakame dust to settle before removing the lid, or you'll lose some of it as it disperses into the air. Store in a covered jar at room temperature.

MAKES 2 TO 3 TABLESPOONS

zippy barbecue sauce

This is a well-balanced barbecue sauce for UnRibs (page 117), tofu, tempeh, or anything else where you want to capture that Fourth of July flavor. It's got just the right amount of sweetness balanced by acidity, heat, and spice. If you prefer your sauce on the sweeter side, feel free to increase the sweetener. (Pictured on page 119.)

2 (6-ounce) cans tomato paste

½ cup maple syrup or organic sugar, or ¾ cup coconut sugar, or more as desired

⅓ cup soy sauce

¼ cup apple cider vinegar

2 tablespoons molasses

½ to 1 teaspoon liquid smoke

6 cloves garlic, minced

2 chipotle peppers in adobo sauce (canned), minced

2 tablespoons chili powder

1 tablespoon smoked paprika

2 teaspoons ground cumin

1 cup water

Combine all of the ingredients in a bowl and whisk together well or mix in a blender or food processor. Store this in a jar in the refrigerator for 2 to 3 months.

MAKES ABOUT 3½ CUPS

no-anchovy worcestershire sauce

Here's a sauce that many can spell but can't pronounce. Whether it's wooster, worster, or wor-ces-ter-sher, the beloved sauce for everything from steak to Bloody Marys was accidentally discovered when a couple of chemists tried to create a seasoning, found it quite nasty, then forgot about it and left it sitting in a barrel for a couple of years. When they dusted off the barrel, they found that their initial unpalatable concoction was now delicious.

For this vegan version, you needn't wait years to sprinkle it on your tofu steak or season your next cocktail. Just 10 minutes.

6 tablespoons soy sauce

½ cup diced onion

¼ cup malt vinegar

2 tablespoons molasses

1 tablespoon tamarind extract

1 sheet nori, torn

3 cloves garlic

¼ teaspoon lemon zest

Pinch of ground cloves

Place all of the ingredients in a blender and puree until smooth. Pour the mixture into a saucepan and simmer over medium-low heat for 5 to 10 minutes. Strain through a sieve, then pour into a jar or bottle. Keep it in the refrigerator for several months.

MAKES ABOUT ¾ CUP

roasted tomatoes and tomato "elixir"

One of my favorite uses for summer's bounty of tomatoes is to roast them. I first tasted them in Provence a number of years ago when buying picnic provisions at a grocery store. Unlike sun-dried tomatoes, which are leathery by virtue of being completely dried out, roasted tomatoes pack a punch in concentrated tomato flavor while remaining tender. They can enhance everything from sandwiches to pastas to appetizers.

Unfortunately, most recipes for roasting tomatoes have you discard the juices and skins. But what a waste! I have found that every aspect of the tomato is glorified by roasting—the resulting juice, which I lovingly call "elixir" (pictured on page 37), is luscious, rich, and sweet, elevating soups, risottos, and sauces, while the skins can be pureed to make a powerful tomato pesto (page 36). And of course, the tomato itself is the star.

If you don't have a bumper crop of tomatoes, make a trip to the farmers' market and pick up a bunch. Make these on a leisurely Sunday afternoon— start to finish is 2 to 3 hours, and while the actual hands-on time is minimal, you have to be around every 20 minutes or so to check the oven.

While the recipe below is more of a methodology than an exact recipe, as it can be easily increased or decreased to your liking, you will want to use at least 10 pounds of good-size tomatoes to make the time involved worthwhile. If you have a convection oven, or two regular ovens, you can likely roast all of them at once; if you have only one oven, you may want to make a smaller amount. Make a bunch and freeze the "elixir," and you'll be able to carry some of summer's flavors into the colder months. The tomatoes themselves, submerged in olive oil, keep for several weeks refrigerated.

⅓ to ½ cup olive oil

8 to 10 pounds ripe medium to large tomatoes

1 head garlic, unpeeled, separated into cloves

Several fresh thyme sprigs (optional; use if available)

Sea salt

continued ﹥

Preheat the oven to 350°F. Line baking sheets with parchment paper or brush them with a little olive oil. Cut the tomatoes in half and place them, cut-side down, on the baking sheets, being careful not to crowd them too much (leave ½ inch or so between the tomatoes). Distribute the garlic cloves and fresh thyme sprigs evenly over the tomatoes and sprinkle on the olive oil. Bake for 20 to 30 minutes, then take the baking sheets out of the oven and very carefully tip them over a bowl, draining as much of the accumulating juices as possible. Do not discard this flavorful liquid—this is the "elixir" that has so many culinary uses! Put the baking sheets back in the oven and continue roasting for another 20 minutes or so, then take out and drain the juices again into the bowl. If the tomato skins are now wrinkly and loose, remove them as well; they should slip off easily with a fork or your fingers (if you can stand the heat). Again, don't discard the skins, as they will be turned into a delicious tomato pesto (page 36).

Sprinkle the tomatoes lightly with salt and return them to the oven. Roast for another 20 minutes and drain, removing any remaining tomato skins, and repeat again a couple of times more, until the tomatoes have become concentrated in size and meaty in texture. Depending on the size and juiciness of the tomatoes, total roasting time will be between 1½ and 2 hours. After cooling, the tomatoes can be stored in the refrigerator for 2 to 3 weeks, in either the drained tomato liquid or olive oil. Keep the highly concentrated, flavorful liquid that you drain during the roasting in the refrigerator for up to 2 weeks or freeze it for several months.

MAKES 1 TO 3 CUPS ROASTED TOMATOES AND ½ TO 2 CUPS "ELIXIR"

HOW TO USE ROASTED TOMATOES AND TOMATO "ELIXIR"

Tomato "Elixir" can be used to replace some of the stock in soups such as minestrone or black bean, while adding oomph. You can enrich pastas or risottos (see Roasted Tomato Risotto, below) with it, cook vegetables in it, or use it to enhance stocks and sauces.

roasted tomato risotto

This is a requisite dish I make at least once every summer, a justification to spend an afternoon roasting tomatoes. Why? Because being temporarily transported to heaven once in a while is something I enjoy. And this gets me there. It is, simply put, luscious. Silky, creamy, rich, capturing the fullness of tomato flavor . . . I could go on and on. But if you're thinking, Sounds great, but I'm not going to stand at the stove stirring for 40 minutes, fear not, because this lovely dish achieves its creaminess all on its own in the oven while you relax with a glass of wine.

One more thing I'd like to add—I find risotto served at American restaurants to be a little too dry. In Italy, risotto is a little looser, with rice suspended in a creamy liquid. This recipe yields the looser texture I like. You'll need to serve it in a shallow bowl instead of a plate, or it may runneth over.

2 tablespoons olive oil

2 onions, minced

1½ cups Arborio rice

6 cups Truly Free-Range Chicken(less) Stock (page 82)

½ cup white wine

6 cloves garlic, minced

½ to 1 teaspoon sea salt

2 cups Roasted Tomatoes (page 33), chopped

1 cup Tomato "Elixir" (page 33)

1 cup loosely packed basil, slivered

Preheat the oven to 350°F. In a large ovenproof pot or Dutch oven over medium heat, heat the oil. Add the onions and sauté until tender. Add the rice and continue to sauté for a couple of minutes. Add the stock, wine, garlic, and ½ teaspoon salt (or more, depending on the saltiness of the stock) and stir. Cover with a lid, put in the oven, and bake for about 20 minutes. Add the tomatoes and tomato elixir and give it a good stir. Put it back in the oven and continue cooking for another 15 minutes or so, until the rice is just al dente and suspended in a lovely, red sauce. Mix in the basil and stir; serve immediately. Pour yourself another glass of wine—a Zinfandel would be nice.

MAKES 6 TO 8 SERVINGS

roasted tomato skin pesto

Those wrinkly tomato skins left over from Roasted Tomatoes (page 33) become a rich pesto that plays beautifully with pasta or polenta, as a spread for sandwiches, or melted into soups. The recipe below is only a guideline, as it is hard to determine exactly the quantity of skins you will end up with.

Approximately 2 cups tomato skins from Roasted Tomatoes (page 33)

Approximately ½ cup olive oil, or more as needed

3 to 6 cloves garlic, peeled

1 tablespoon white or yellow miso, or 1 teaspoon sea salt

Place all of the ingredients in a blender and puree until smooth, thick, and spreadable. Start with the lesser amount of garlic, as you can always increase it depending on how garlicky you like it. The sauce will thicken even more as it sits. This flavorful pesto can be refrigerated in a jar for 3 to 4 weeks or frozen for up to 1 year. Pouring a layer of olive oil on top of the pesto will keep it fresher for even longer than 4 weeks in the fridge.

MAKES ½ TO 1 CUP

Roasted Tomato Skin Pesto and
Tomato "Elixir" (page 33)

that bottle of italian dressing

I grew up in a house without bottled salad dressing. A salad at our house was always dressed with simple vinaigrette. Bor-ing. All my friends seemed to have not just one, but several bottles of commercial salad dressing in their fridge. At their house, salad was my favorite food. So this is my tribute to that ubiquitous bottle of Italian dressing that I dreamt about—only it's better.

1½ cups extra-virgin olive oil

½ cup red wine vinegar

3 to 4 tablespoons Dijon Mustard (page 21) or a store-bought variety

⅓ cup nutritional yeast

3 tablespoons agave or organic sugar

1 teaspoon sea salt

2 teaspoons dried basil

2 teaspoons dried oregano

1 teaspoon dried thyme

1 teaspoon dried rosemary

1 teaspoon dried marjoram

½ teaspoon freshly ground black pepper

Add all of the ingredients to a glass jar and shake until combined. Use more Dijon mustard if you like it zesty. This keeps in the refrigerator for 4 to 6 weeks.

MAKES ABOUT 2½ CUPS

ranch dressing

Here is an oil-free rendition of the classic dressing and dip that's so easy to make at home. The variation that follows is richer and based on mayonnaise.

½ cup cashews

½ cup water

¼ cup freshly squeezed lemon juice

8 ounces medium, medium-firm, or soft tofu, crumbled

1 tablespoon Dijon Mustard (page 21) or a store-bought variety

2 tablespoons chopped onion

2 cloves garlic

1 teaspoon dried dill, or 1 tablespoon fresh dill

1 teaspoon sea salt

½ teaspoon freshly ground black pepper

Place the cashews, water, and lemon juice in a blender and puree until smooth. Add the remaining ingredients and process until creamy. Store the dressing in a jar in the fridge for up to 2 weeks.

MAKES ABOUT 2 CUPS

VARIATION

EXTRA-THICK AND CREAMY RANCH DRESSING Replace the cashews and water with 1 cup of Classic Eggless Mayonnaise (page 16). Simply puree everything in a blender until creamy.

creamy no-oil caesar dressing

Why use oil when you really don't have to? This creamy Caesar dressing will not leave anyone wanting.

3 ounces medium, medium-firm, regular, or silken tofu

⅓ cup water

⅓ cup freshly squeezed lemon juice

3 tablespoons soy sauce

3 tablespoons Dijon Mustard (page 21) or a store-bought variety

3 tablespoons almond meal

3 tablespoons nutritional yeast

1 tablespoon balsamic vinegar

½ sheet nori

4 cloves garlic

Put all of the ingredients in a blender and process until creamy. You can add more garlic, depending on how garlicky you like it. Store in the refrigerator for up to 2 weeks.

MAKES ABOUT 2 CUPS

not-tella chocolate hazelnut spread

This makes a rich, chocolaty spread that is the adult answer to, well, you know, that other stuff. Spread it on bread or bananas or just take a big spoonful and lick yourself to heaven.

2 cups hazelnuts

4 ounces dark chocolate (60% or higher)

3 tablespoons refined coconut oil

⅓ cup organic sugar

6 tablespoons Dutch-processed cocoa powder

Preheat the oven to 300°F. Spread the hazelnuts on a baking sheet and roast for about 15 minutes, until lightly browned. Let them cool. Using a towel, rub off most of the loose skins.

Melt the chocolate and coconut oil together in a double boiler or in the microwave. If melting in the microwave, microwave for 1 minute, stir, then repeat for another 30 seconds.

Put the hazelnuts and the sugar in a blender and process until pulverized and the mixture begins to get oily. It should start to be pasty, and no chunks should remain. Add the chocolate mixture and cocoa powder, and continue to process until very creamy. It will be runny but will thicken when refrigerated for a day. If stored at room temperature, it will take several days to thicken to a spreadable consistency. Keep the spread in a jar in the pantry for 4 to 6 weeks, if it lasts that long!

MAKES ABOUT 2 CUPS

any-fruit chutney

Chutneys range from sweet and spicy to sour and salty and can be made from an enormous range of fruits and vegetables. But for the purposes of this book, let's focus on Chutney 101, where it is basically made like jam with spices and an acidic ingredient thrown in. Choose any fruit to be your base. In the fall, when the bumper crop of figs and Asian pears comes into our garden, chutney is one of the things I make with them. You can make it with nontraditional fruit, as I do, or stick with the more traditional ones like mangoes. I've provided a range of some of the ingredients so that you can adjust them according to the fruit and your liking, but the general directions are the same. In using it, go beyond curries and add it to sandwiches, serve it with vegan cheese and crackers, or use it as a topping for hors d'oeuvres.

---

2 pounds fresh fruit (such as figs, mangoes, apples, Asian pears, persimmons, berries), peeled if necessary

⅓ to ½ cup organic sugar

¼ cup apple cider vinegar or freshly squeezed lemon juice, or more as needed

2 teaspoons grated fresh ginger

1 teaspoon coriander seeds

½ to 1 teaspoon sea salt

1 dried chile, or more as needed

Dice the fruit into ⅓-inch pieces. Combine the fruit with ⅓ cup sugar (or more, depending on how sweet you like it) and the vinegar, ginger, coriander, salt, and chile in a saucepan over medium heat and bring to a boil. Turn down the heat and simmer, stirring occasionally, for 30 to 40 minutes, until reduced by about half. As the chutney cooks down, taste it and see if the flavors are balanced. If too sweet, add a little more vinegar or lemon juice, or throw in another chile pepper if you prefer it spicier.

If you want to store all of your chutney in the refrigerator, you can just let it cool and store in a jar for several months. But if you want to store it in your pantry, you'll need to hot-pack it. This is easy. Wash some jars in hot, soapy water and rinse well. Pack the hot chutney in the jars, making sure to leave ½ inch of space at the top; don't let it cool down before you pack it! Then put the lid on securely. You don't need to pressure-cook it if you pack jams and chutneys hot.

MAKES 3 CUPS

jam: the easy, cheat method

Who says you have to boil jams and jellies for hours, or deal with pectin, an ingredient you may or may not be familiar with? Jam is essentially a thick, sweet fruit sauce, so does it really matter how it's made if it still tastes great on toast? I say no, and therefore offer up this idiotproof method that we used to make at my old restaurant with whatever fruit we happened to have. It works great with frozen fruit, such as raspberries, blueberries, or strawberries, and can be made in small batches so that your jam is always fresh. Basically, the fruit is combined with a sweetener (either sugar or fruit juice concentrate), then simmered briefly, and finally thickened with a bit of arrowroot. That's it, and it tastes so fruity!

12 ounces raspberries, blueberries, strawberries, pitted cherries, or other fruit of choice, either fresh or frozen

¼ to ⅓ cup organic sugar, or 1 cup frozen apple or white grape juice concentrate

1 tablespoon arrowroot, or 2 tablespoons arrowroot if using juice concentrate

2 tablespoons water

Combine the fruit and sweetener (use more or less sugar depending on how sweet you like it) in a medium saucepan over medium-low heat and bring to a simmer. Simmer for 10 to 20 minutes, until the fruit has broken down a bit and the mixture looks saucy. Dissolve the arrowroot in the water, and whisk into the fruit mixture. It will thicken some but not be quite as thick as jam. Pour the jam into a container or a pretty dish or hot-pack it in a Mason jar: Wash some jars in hot, soapy water and rinse well. Pack the hot jam in the jars, making sure to leave ½ inch of space at the top; don't let it cool down before you pack it! Then put the lid on securely. As it cools, it will thicken into a jammy consistency. This quick jam will keep for 2 to 3 weeks in the refrigerator if placed in a dish or regular jar, and 6 to 8 weeks if packed hot.

MAKES ABOUT 1 CUP

grape and wine jelly

Here's a grape jelly that changes all the rules about PB&J. Enhanced with a touch of wine, it adds a hint of sophistication to the usual. My husband, an amateur wine maker, grows heavenly Cabernet grapes but sometimes gets too busy to make wine, leaving me with the task of turning them into something else. Although you can make this with any grape juice (even bottled), if you happen to pass a vineyard, I say ask if you can pluck a few bunches for some adult jam.

---

6 cups grape juice, freshly pressed or bottled

1½ cups organic sugar

¾ cup dry red wine

6 tablespoons arrowroot

¼ cup water

Combine the grape juice, sugar, and wine in a large, heavy pot or Dutch oven over medium heat and bring to a boil. Turn down the heat and simmer, uncovered, for about 1 hour, until it has reduced by half and become the consistency of light syrup. Dissolve the arrowroot in the water, and whisk it into the jelly. Simmer for another minute until it bubbles and thickens. Pack hot: Wash some jars in hot, soapy water and rinse well. Pack the hot jam in the jars, making sure to leave ½ inch of space at the top; don't let it cool down before you pack it! Then put the lid on securely. It should keep in your cupboard unopened for up to 1 year. Once opened, keep in the refrigerator for a couple of months.

MAKES 3 CUPS

fig and lavender jam

My garden is graced by two magnificent fig trees that produce a bounty of purple jewels each year. I fill my belly snacking on them each day during fig season and make everything under the sun that I can think of, using them in salads, cold soups, sauces, and smoothies. But the trees just keep on giving and giving. So I make jam. Around the same time, my garden is filled with fragrant lavender, and its flowers go into the jam, too, adding an incomparable layer of floral flavor.

4 pounds fresh figs, cut into ½-inch pieces

1½ cups organic sugar

2 to 4 tablespoons fresh lavender flowers

Put the figs in a large, heavy pot and add the sugar. Bring to a boil over medium heat, then turn down the heat to very low and give them a long, slow, loving cooking, stirring often with a big, wooden spoon to get to the bottom of the pot to make sure it doesn't burn. It will take 1 hour to 90 minutes to cook down and reduce by a third to a half, when it will start to look like jam, thick and syrupy. At this point, add the lavender flowers and cook for another 10 to 15 minutes.

Toward the end of the cooking, prepare your jars. Bring a big pot of water to a boil and immerse in it any jar with a tight-fitting lid—they don't all have to be Mason jars, and I usually have a motley selection of shapes and sizes. Just keep in mind that you'll need enough jars for 6 cups of jam, so depending on the size of your jars, you'll need more or fewer. Boil the jars for about 5 minutes, then keep them in the pot of water until the jam is ready.

When the jam is finished, use tongs to remove one jar at a time. Fill the jars with the jam, leaving ½ inch of space at the top. Put the lid on and tighten it. Fill all the jars in the same way. If done properly, you'll hear a "pop" of the lid in a few minutes. It's all very easy to do, so don't be afraid you didn't do it right. Keep it in a cool pantry, where it should be good until the next harvest season. Once opened, it will keep in your refrigerator for a couple of months.

MAKES 6 CUPS

dairy- and egg-free goodness

It wasn't long ago when giving up dairy and eggs meant giving up a big chunk of what our culture eats. Now, with the plethora of dairy and egg alternatives available on the market, vegans have no trouble re-creating every long-forgotten treasure from their past.

But many of the dairy alternatives available on the market are highly processed, not what we want to be putting into our bodies every day. And most contain palm oil or its derivatives, such as vitamin A palmitate. Palm oil plantations are rapidly displacing rain forests and, with that, endangered species such as orangutans, tigers, and rhinos, decimating their populations and ravaging ecosystems and biodiversity. When animals are destroyed and displaced, I have to ask the question: is palm oil really vegan? But I don't want just to condemn. I want to be able to offer a solution—alternatives for you to enjoy, even better than the ones you can buy at the store.

Whether it's a creamer for your coffee, a viable solution for your morning toast, or a heavy cream substitute that really whips, you'll find it here. And what about things that even the manufacturers haven't figured out, like meringue? You'll find that here, too. And there's cheese, of course, everyone's Holy Grail. I've developed new recipes for easy, meltable cheeses that contain no oil. And best of all, they're quick and easy, so you'll find yourself making them again and again.

creamy soy milk with no beany flavor

There are few options for commercial soy milks that are unadulterated. Most are flavored, sugared, and thickened with carrageenan or other things. So if you're looking to increase the purity of your pantry, making your own soy milk might be a great option.

If you're going to make this on a regular basis, investing in an inexpensive soy milk maker will make the job a whole lot easier. But it's still possible to do it without any special equipment (after all, people have been drinking soy milk in Asia for centuries). Also, if your only exposure to soy milk is the commercial variety, you might be surprised by the flavor of traditionally made homemade soy milk and its fresh, beany character—loved by some, hated by others. While some of that can be masked by a little salt and sweetener, it does not entirely eliminate it. I began to wonder—how do the commercial manufacturers eliminate the beany taste? By digging around some industry papers online, I learned that an enzyme responsible for the beany flavor was triggered by exposure to cold water during the soaking process. Heat, on the other hand, killed it. So the trick was to minimize the unpalatable enzyme by exposing it to heat. In English: Don't soak the beans before cooking them.

This soy milk is fairly neutral in flavor without an overwhelming beany taste. Of course, you can enhance the flavor of your soy milk by adding a squirt of vanilla, a tablespoon or two of sweetener, or a dash of salt. But it is more than palatable as it is, and it even foams when used in making a cappuccino! A nut milk bag is preferable for this, but you may also use a sieve lined with a triple layer of cheesecloth. After straining the soy milk, you'll be left with a dry pulp called okara. See the sidebar on page 52 for recipes that use okara.

About 14 cups water

1½ cups dry soybeans, unsoaked

1 teaspoon vanilla extract, 1 tablespoon organic sugar or maple syrup, and/or a pinch of salt, for flavoring (optional)

continued >

Bring 8 cups of the water to a boil in a pot. Add the soybeans and boil for 1 minute. Remove from the heat and let sit for 30 minutes. At that point, the water should be cool enough to touch. Drain the soybeans, then transfer half to a blender with 3 cups of the remaining water. Briefly blend until it forms a thick slurry. Be sure not to blend long—just 10 to 20 seconds should be enough.

Pour this slurry through the nut milk bag or sieve into a bowl or container. Squeeze the nut milk bag or press the contents in the sieve with a wooden spoon to extract as much of the milk as possible and leave the remaining pulp as dry as possible. Repeat this blending and straining process with the remaining soybeans and 3 cups water. Pour the soy milk into a large pot and bring to a simmer over medium heat; turn down the heat and continue to simmer at a heat level that will not boil over for 5 to 10 minutes. It's now done. If you like, flavor it with vanilla, a pinch of salt, and sweetener. You can let it cool, then transfer to a container of choice. Stored this way, it keeps in the refrigerator for 3 to 4 days.

To lengthen the shelf life of the soy milk, pour it while it's hot into clean, wide-mouthed jars, cover with lids, and store in the refrigerator. Unopened, it will keep for almost 3 weeks. After opening, it will keep for 5 to 7 days.

MAKES 4 CUPS

HOW TO USE OKARA

Now that you've made soy milk, you'll have a couple of cups of okara, the high-fiber by-product. What can you do with it? Okara adds a flaky texture to foods, so it's a perfect addition to things like "fish" or nuggets. Check out the recipe for San Francisco Fab Cakes with Capers (page 109), Gold Nuggets (page 114), or UnFish Sticks (page 107). You can also add it to muffins and breads as a partial flour substitute and to add fiber, or mix it into your dog's food. If you have other critters, like chickens, they love it, too! Store okara in the refrigerator for 1 week or in the freezer for 1 year.

cashew milk

Because of the high ratio of water to cashews in this recipe, there's no need to soak the cashews unless your blender is particularly weak. This makes it a great option when you've run out of a nondairy milk in the fridge and need something in a hurry! Unlike almond or soy milk, there's also no straining involved, so it's easy and instant!

4 cups water

½ to ⅔ cup cashews

4 to 6 soaked dates, pitted, or 1 tablespoon sweetener such as sugar, maple syrup, or brown rice syrup (optional)

1 teaspoon vanilla extract (optional)

Place the water, ½ cup cashews (or more, depending on how rich you like it), sweetener, and vanilla in a blender and process on high for about 1 minute, until smooth and creamy. There should be no hint of graininess or residue left, but if there is, pour the milk through a sieve or nut milk bag. Store this covered in the refrigerator for 4 to 7 days.

MAKES 4 CUPS

almond milk and coffee creamer

This is a two-for-one recipe—in other words, you get milk and creamer at the same time. If you just want one or the other, you can do that, although I like to make both of them at the same time. Almonds make delicious milk, as most people know, but with a little less water, they are a great base for coffee creamer. So save yourself some time and trouble, and make both at once!

For ultimate smoothness, I highly recommend purchasing an inexpensive nut milk bag. While you can use a sieve with cheesecloth for straining, you risk getting some of the pulp in the milk.

---

2 cups raw almonds, soaked for at least 8 hours in water

6 cups water

4 to 6 soaked dates, pitted, or 1 tablespoon sweetener such as sugar, maple syrup, or brown rice syrup (optional)

½ teaspoon vanilla, hazelnut, or other extract, or more, for custom flavors (optional)

Before you begin, have on hand a nut milk bag and a large bowl, or a large bowl with a sieve placed over it. Line the sieve with two or three layers of cheesecloth.

Drain and rinse the almonds. Put them in a blender with 4 cups of the water (you may have to do this in two batches if your blender is small) and the soaked dates, if you are using them for sweetness. Process this for a couple of minutes until smooth and creamy. Pour the mixture into the nut milk bag or over the lined sieve, and let it drain into the bowl. If you are using the nut milk bag, start squeezing gently to extract as much of the milk as possible. If you're using the sieve, let it drain as much as possible, then use a wooden spoon or rubber spatula to press out as much milk as possible.

This is now the coffee creamer. Remove 1 cup of it and store it in a jar for use in coffee or other hot beverages. To make milk with the remaining mixture, simply dilute it with the remaining 2 cups water. If you prefer a sweetened or flavored beverage, add more sweetener of choice and a few drops of vanilla or other extract. Store covered in the refrigerator, where it will stay fresh for 5 to 7 days.

MAKES 4 CUPS MILK AND 1 CUP CREAMER

cashew cream

Cashew cream helped wean me off of dairy over thirty years ago. I was addicted to cooking with heavy cream, and this alone proved to be a rich and satisfying substitute. Oh, sweet cashew, how can I sing thy praises? You add richness, creaminess, and a silky mouthfeel to everything from soups and sauces to desserts. Wherever heavy cream might once have gone, you, cashew cream, tread there now!

This is the base of many a decadent meal. The lovely thing about it is how thick and creamy it gets when heated, without any of the fuss of making a roux and using all that oil and flour. Thus, it translates beautifully into everything from a classic béchamel to a quick Alfredo. Use it wherever heavy cream is called for in a recipe.

---

3 cups water

1 cup cashews

Place the water and cashews in a blender and blend until smooth and creamy, about 1 minute. That's it! The cream keeps in the refrigerator for 1 to 3 days.

Note: For a thicker cream, reduce the water by $1/2$ cup.

MAKES ABOUT 3½ CUPS

HOW TO USE CASHEW CREAM

To make a classic white sauce (béchamel), simply heat the cashew cream in a saucepan until thick and creamy, seasoning well with salt, pepper, and a grating of nutmeg. It will thicken on its own without the addition of any flour, cornstarch, or other starch. For Alfredo, season with garlic, nutritional yeast, salt, pepper, and a splash or two of white wine. For a mushroom sauce, sauté some sliced mushrooms, then add the cashew cream and cook until thickened. If you like, add a dash or two of sherry or Madeira and season well with salt and pepper.

cashew or almond crème fraîche

A bit lighter than sour cream, crème fraîche is a wonderful topping for soups, desserts, and appetizers. This one is made by culturing cashews or almonds with a bit of nondairy yogurt. If using almonds, you'll need a nut milk bag or a sieve lined with two or three layers of cheesecloth.

1 cup cashews or raw almonds, soaked in water for at least 8 hours

¾ cup water if using cashews, or 1¼ cups water if using almonds

¼ cup plain nondairy yogurt, homemade (page 60) or a store-bought variety

¼ teaspoon sea salt

TO USE CASHEWS:
Puree the nuts, water, yogurt, and salt in a blender until smooth. Pour this into a clean container, cover with a lid, and set at room temperature for 24 to 72 hours, until thickened and sour. Refrigerate the mixture, where it will get slightly thicker after a day. Cashew Crème Fraîche will keep in the refrigerator for 2 to 3 weeks.

TO USE ALMONDS:
Puree the almonds and water in a blender until a creamy sludge forms. Pour this into a nut milk bag or over a lined sieve and let it drain into a bowl. Gently squeeze the nut milk bag to extract as much of the milk as possible or use a wooden spoon or rubber spatula to press as much milk as possible through the sieve. Stir in the yogurt and salt. Cover with a lid or plastic wrap and set at room temperature for 24 to 72 hours, until thickened and sour. Refrigerate the mixture, where it will get slightly thicker after a day. Almond Crème Fraîche will keep in the refrigerator for 2 to 3 weeks.

MAKES ABOUT 2 CUPS

glorious butterless butter

I once reeled with shock when I saw a French girl spread butter as thick as cheese on her toast—until I tried it. Then I understood. Butter, glorious butter! Not only does it impart incomparable flavor and texture to baked goods and dishes, but on toast—well, it doesn't get any better. Now for the times when I want a hard butter for flaky croissants, or an unsalted butter for a fluffy buttercream, or a light, whipped one for scones, I make my own non-dairy butter. And then I have to put a lock on it so I don't eat it all up!

This recipe can be adjusted to suit your taste or purpose. Be sure to check out the variations on the opposite page. Don't use extra-virgin coconut oil, or it will taste like coconuts.

1½ cups melted refined coconut oil (not extra-virgin coconut oil)

½ cup Creamy Soy Milk with No Beany Flavor (page 51), Almond Milk (page 54), Cashew Milk (page 53), or Cashew Cream (page 56), or store-bought nondairy milk

¼ cup canola, grapeseed, or light olive oil

½ teaspoon sea salt

2 teaspoons liquid lecithin (see sidebar)

Place all of the ingredients in a blender and process at medium speed for about 1 minute. Pour into a container of your choice—something made of silicone is great, as it will pop out easily, but any storage container will do (line it with wax paper first for easy removal). Set it in the refrigerator for a few hours until hard or in the freezer to expedite hardening. This glorious butter substitute will keep in the refrigerator for 3 to 4 weeks or many months in the freezer.

MAKES 1 POUND (ABOUT 2 CUPS)

LECITHIN

Lecithin is an emulsifying agent generally derived from soybeans. It will help mix oil and water and prevent separation. If you can find only lecithin granules, you'll need to use two to four times the amount of the liquid lecithin called for.

VARIATIONS

CULTURED BUTTER Replace the nondairy milk with ½ cup plain nondairy yogurt, or add 1 teaspoon of apple cider vinegar or lemon juice to the nondairy milk.

REALLY HARD BUTTER This is helpful for making puff pastry, croissants, and the like. Increase the coconut oil to 2½ cups or substitute deodorized cocoa butter for ½ cup of the coconut oil.

WHIPPED BUTTER Increase the canola oil by 1 tablespoon and process at high speed in the blender for about 2 minutes to incorporate as much air as possible.

UNSALTED BUTTER This is often called for in buttercreams and some desserts. Simply omit the salt!

Glorious Butterless Butter and
Fluffy Biscuits (page 160)

nice, thick nondairy yogurt

There is no mystery to making yogurt at home: you need something containing live cultures (either a commercial nondairy yogurt or a pack of dry cultures), some type of nondairy milk, a warm place to culture it, and enough patience to wait 8 hours or so. While a yogurt maker is helpful, it's not necessary—after all, humankind has been making yogurt for thousands of years.

Soy yogurt is the easiest to make, as the proteins in the soy milk help thicken it beautifully. Other nondairy milks can present a problem in terms of thickening properly. While they will culture and get tangy, they often stay runny in consistency. Commercial yogurt manufacturers often add a variety of stabilizers and thickeners to almond yogurt and coconut yogurt in order to achieve that creamy, thick mouthfeel and texture. Luckily, we can replicate this at home by adding a little agar or pectin and a little arrowroot. Or you can borrow a tip from my friend, blogger Stephanie Weaver, who solves the problem by adding chia seeds, which also boost fiber and nutritional content (see Variations, opposite).

4 cups Almond Milk (page 54) or store-bought almond or coconut milk beverage

⅓ cup cashews (see Note, page 62)

2 tablespoons arrowroot or cornstarch

¼ teaspoon agar powder, or 1 teaspoon low-sugar pectin

2 tablespoons store-bought plain soy yogurt, or ¼ cup store-bought coconut yogurt, or 1 teaspoon or 1 packet commercial nondairy yogurt culture (available online)

1 teaspoon vanilla extract (optional)

1 tablespoon agave, organic sugar, or maple syrup (optional)

Place the almond milk, cashews, arrowroot, and agar in a blender and process until smooth and creamy. Pour this into a 2-quart saucepan over medium heat and bring to a simmer. Cook for 3 to 4 minutes, until thick. Pour the mixture into a 1-quart jar and let it rest and cool until the temperature drops to 110°F. Gently stir in the nondairy yogurt. Add the vanilla and sweetener. Put the lid on the jar and maintain a temperature of 105°F to 110°F (see sidebar, page 62, for tips) for 6 to 8 hours, until thick and tangy. This yogurt will thicken further after refrigeration. Serve with

continued >

VARIATIONS

CHIA SEED YOGURT Omit the
arrowroot and agar or pectin. Simply
heat the milk to 110°F (no need to
simmer), and then stir in 3 tablespoons
of chia seeds with the yogurt.

THICK SOY MILK YOGURT Replace the
almond milk with soy milk and increase
the cashews to 1 cup.

the toppings of your choice (cherries and granola are pictured here). Homemade yogurt will keep for about 2 weeks in your refrigerator.

Note: The cashews can be omitted if desired, but they help thicken and enrich the yogurt.

MAKES 4 CUPS

YOGURT TIPS AND RECOMMENDED EQUIPMENT

Before you go out and spend a lot of money on a yogurt maker, think about this fact: humans have been making yogurt for thousands of years without a lot of technology. However, you must keep in mind that the yogurt must maintain a temperature of around 110°F for 6 to 8 hours in order for the lactic acid bacteria to grow sufficiently to make it tangy and thick. So think about what you have in your house that will do that. It's a lot easier than you might imagine—I make yogurt outside on warm days, simply wrapping my jars in a few towels and setting them out in the sun. Or you can use a dehydrator, a slow cooker or rice cooker partially filled with water (place the jars in the cooker, and pour water around them almost to the top), an oven turned on and off every hour or so, an electric blanket, or a blanket next to a heater or fireplace. Whichever of these methods you choose to use, I do recommend getting an inexpensive thermometer so you can measure the temperature of the milk.

amazing cultured creamless sour cream

A thick dollop of buttery, tangy cream is not one of those things that can be achieved by pureeing tofu with lemon juice (okay, so I made tofu sour cream for a long time, too). The best sour cream is cultured by encouraging lactic acid growth in a plant-based cream. Culturing full-fat coconut milk produces a sour cream that is so rich and tangy you won't believe it's not the other stuff!

1 (13.5-ounce) can full-fat coconut milk

2 tablespoons nondairy yogurt, homemade (page 60) or a store-bought variety

Combine the coconut milk with the yogurt in a bowl or jar and cover with a lid or plastic wrap, nothing permeable. Keep at room temperature for 24 to 72 hours, until it is sour in flavor (yes, dip a spoon in it and taste it). It will still be softer than sour cream at this point, but it should taste like sour cream. Put it in the refrigerator for 24 hours, where it will thicken considerably. It is now ready to serve. Coconut sour cream can be kept refrigerated in a jar for 2 to 3 weeks.

MAKES ABOUT 2 CUPS

VARIATION

FAST TRACK METHOD Heat the coconut milk on the stove to 110°F. If you don't have a thermometer, do the "wrist test," where a few drops on your wrist feel warm but not hot (just like when you're preparing a bottle for a baby). Pour it into a jar and stir in the yogurt. Affix the lid. Now, the trick is to maintain a temperature of 105°F to 110°F for 8 to 12 hours. You can do this by wrapping it in a puffy jacket or blanket, setting it in a dehydrator, wrapping it in towels and setting it next to a heater, or immersing the jar in a rice or slow cooker partially filled with water. You can also use a yogurt maker. Somewhere in your house, there is a warm location where you can maintain the temperature. Taste it and, when it is sufficiently sour, transfer it to the refrigerator, where it will thicken after a day to the consistency of sour cream.

flax seed egg whites

Sure, ground flax seeds are often mixed with water to function as an egg substitute in many vegan baking applications, but add too much, and you've got flax seed-flavored cake. Here is a way of harnessing the amazing power of flax seeds while leaving the funky flavor behind.

Best of all, there's no waste. After you cook the flax seeds and strain them, you'll use the resulting goop as "meringue" and turn the strained flax seeds into delicate gluten-free crackers. It's hard to beat (except for the meringue)! A word to the wise, however: this recipe can be a bit fussy, and some people have a harder time than others in getting it to work.

---

3 cups water

⅓ cup whole flax seeds, brown or golden

Combine the water and flax seeds in a medium saucepan. For this particular application, I've found that a wider saucepan works better than a narrow one (this was discovered after many attempts—it helps cook the flax seeds properly to create the right viscosity). Bring to a boil over medium heat, then turn down the heat and simmer for 10 to 15 minutes, until the liquid is bubbly and has reduced by about half to two-thirds. It will be somewhat thick and gloppy looking. Place a sieve over a bowl and strain the mixture through it, using a spatula to stir the seeds around and help them drain. (Reserve the flax seeds for the Delicate Flax Seed Crackers, page 171.) You should have about ½ cup. If you have much more than that, put the goop and seeds back in the pan and cook some more to reduce it (slightly more than ½ cup is fine), then re-strain. It will look slightly thicker than raw egg whites and, as it chills, will get even goopier and thicker. Put the goop in a jar and store in the refrigerator for up to 1 week, or freeze for 3 to 4 months. To use it for whipping, it will need to be chilled overnight or, better yet, frozen. However, it can be used right away for baking applications.

Note: If the goop has thickened too much and won't strain, put the seeds back in the pan and add another ½ cup of water. Bring to a simmer briefly, then try straining again. Alternatively, you can boil down and reduce the strained flax seed goop to the correct viscosity (for example, if you have strained 1 cup, you can boil that down to ½ cup). Also, make sure that you are using new flax seeds. In other words, if your flax seeds have been in your cupboard for a year, they could be rancid and be not only unhealthy, but simply not work. Get fresh seeds from the store for best results.

MAKES ABOUT ½ CUP "GOOP," FOR 4 CUPS MERINGUE

HOW TO USE FLAX SEED EGG WHITES

Flax seed egg whites whip up like egg whites (see page 67), can be baked into meringues and Pavlovas, and may be folded into puddings and mousses to add incomparable lightness. And it works to bind as well, lending crispness and leavening to certain baked goods and omelets.

flax seed omelets, frittata, and quiche

I learned to make omelets out of Julia Child's *Mastering the Art of French Cooking*. During a period in my life when I was enamored with French cuisine, I literally cracked egg after egg, perfecting the skill of making a creamy omelet in less than 60 seconds. This mixture is the closest vegan substitute I've found to the French style of omelet—golden brown on the outside, tender and creamy on the inside, somewhat lacy on the edges, and a little thinner than American style. But don't stop at just omelets; this makes delicate frittatas and quiches as well, baking up golden brown, studded with whatever lovely veggies and delights you can tuck into it.

1 pound regular or medium tofu

½ cup Flax Seed Egg Whites (page 64)

1 tablespoon nutritional yeast

1 teaspoon black salt (kala namak; see sidebar, page 16)

Pinch of turmeric, for color

Combine all of the ingredients in a food processor and process until smooth and creamy.

OMELET
To cook omelets, heat a nonstick pan and coat lightly with vegetable oil or melt some Glorious Butterless Butter (page 58). When the pan is nice and hot, spoon on some of the mixture, spreading with a spatula to

continued ➣

a ¼-inch thickness. Cover with a lid and cook over medium-low heat for about 5 minutes, until bubbles form and the top looks relatively dry. Put your choice of fillings on one side and use a spatula to fold it over and out onto a plate.

FRITTATA

To bake a frittata, combine the mixture with sautéed vegetables of your choice, grated vegan cheese, or whatever you fancy. Pour the mixture into an oiled quiche pan or 8 by 8-inch baking dish and bake at 350°F for about 45 minutes, until puffy and golden brown.

QUICHE

Combine the mixture with a sautéed onion and veggies of your choice, grated vegan cheese, or other delights. Pour the mixture into a prepared pie crust and bake at 350°F for 45 minutes, until puffy and golden brown.

MAKES 6 TO 8 OMELETS, OR 1 LARGE FRITTATA OR QUICHE

flax seed meringue

Do you dream of fluffy meringue that could be inserted between the words lemon and pie? How about crispy white meringue cookies that dissolve in your mouth? Or of somehow infusing air into often all-too-heavy vegan puddings and mousses? Meet flax seed meringue. This is indeed like a science experiment. It is almost unbelievable that this strange goop whips up into beautiful white clouds of meringue. This is most easily made with an electric mixer, although whipping with a whisk can be a very effective, albeit tiring, way of building forearm muscles.

½ cup Flax Seed Egg Whites (page 64) or more, frozen overnight or longer

⅓ to ½ cup organic granulated or powdered sugar

½ to 1 teaspoon xanthan gum

A few drops of lemon oil or almond extract or a dash of cocoa powder, or ground cinnamon, for flavoring (optional)

Thaw the flax seed egg whites at room temperature for 30 minutes to an hour until it can be broken up into chunks. Using an electric mixer, whip the partly frozen whites on high speed for 3 to 5 minutes, until it increases about eightfold and is light, white, and fluffy like soft meringue. If you have not frozen the whites (but they have been refrigerated overnight), they will take two to three times as long to whip up. Add ⅓ cup sugar (or more, if you like it sweeter) and continue whipping for about another minute or two until fairly stiff. Add ½ teaspoon xanthan gum. The mixture should form stiff peaks; if not, add the remaining ½ teaspoon of xanthan gum and whip again briefly. Add the optional flavorings at this time, depending on what you're making (I love lemon oil for meringue cookies!). It's best to use flax seed meringue immediately. The whipped meringue will hold up for a day or so in the fridge, although it can deflate quickly sometimes.

MAKES 4 TO 6 CUPS

HOW TO USE FLAX SEED MERINGUE

You can use flax seed meringue in any recipe calling for folding in raw, whipped egg whites, such as mousses, chiffons, and cold soufflés. And there's no risk of salmonella! To bake into cookies or meringue shells, follow the instructions on page 69.

continued ⌖

flax seed meringue cookies

I'd been making flax seed meringue for 30 years, but it always seemed to collapse under heat. Then someone discovered my blog post about it, and a forum thread started on *Post Punk Kitchen*. There, Loomi discovered that it would stand up to low heat, and meringue cookies were created! They can be tricky, however, and their baking times can range quite a bit, so be prepared. The most surefire way to bake them is overnight at 150°F to 200°F, or even use a dehydrator at a high setting. You can bake them at a slightly higher temperature (250°F) in about 3 hours, but depending on their size, the middle might be a bit gooey or they could be hollow inside.

4 to 6 cups Flax Seed Meringue (page 67; make using the ½ cup sugar)

For best results (if you are not using a dehydrator), preheat the oven to 150°F to 200°F. For faster results, preheat the oven to 250°F. Line baking sheets with parchment paper. Put the whipped meringue mixture (use the entire batch of the Flax Seed Meringue) into a pastry bag fitted with a medium or large star tip. Pipe onto the parchment paper–lined sheets into cute little meringue cookies, squiggly lines, or any shape you like. You can also just drop them onto the pan with a spoon. Please note that these meringues do not keep their shape as well as chicken egg whites, so if you use a star tip, your cookies could just be round without the edges, although a lower temperature will help maintain shape better than a high one (I have successfully baked meringue cookies with ridges at lower temperatures). In a dehydrator on the highest setting or in an oven at 150°F to 200°F, bake for 6 to 12 hours, until they are completely dry throughout (they are hard to overbake at this low temperature, so you needn't worry too much about that). This is a good recipe to start at night so you can bake while you sleep! At 250°F, bake for about 3 hours (check to make sure the center is not moist or hollow), then turn off the heat and let them sit in the oven for another hour to dry completely. They should be completely dry, light, and crispy. Cool completely before storing in an airtight container or ziplock bag, where they will keep for 2 to 3 months at room temperature or in the refrigerator. They will stay crisp as long as there is no moisture in the bag.

MAKES 24 TO 36 COOKIES (RECIPE MAY BE DOUBLED)

oil-free melty "pepper jack"

When I finally figured out how to make an oil-free cheese that melted, I was thrilled. Now I can feel good about grilled cheese sandwiches and enchiladas (and so can you)! This is still a cultured cheese, which means that from start to finish, you'll need about 3 days, although the hands-on time is only about 10 minutes.

1 cup cashews

1 cup Easy Rejuvelac (recipe follows) or juice from sauerkraut

1 teaspoon sea salt

2 jalapeños, or equivalent of jarred jalapeños

½ cup plus 2 tablespoons water

1 tablespoon agar powder

2 tablespoons tapioca

Puree the cashews, rejuvelac, and salt in a blender until smooth. Transfer to a clean container or jar, cover with a lid, and let sit at room temperature for 1 or 2 days, until the mixture has thickened, risen, and formed air pockets and is tangy. The texture will also have changed, and it will be somewhat gooey and thick.

Preheat the oven to 425°F. Roast the jalapeños in the oven for about 20 minutes until puffy and charred, or grill over an open flame until charred. Wash or rub off the charred part, then split them in half and scrape out and discard the seeds. Finely dice the jalapeños. (If you're using canned jalapeños, you need not roast—just dice them.)

Put the ½ cup water in a small saucepan with the agar powder and whisk it well. Cover the pot with a lid and bring to a simmer over low heat. Don't peek for 3 to 4 minutes, then check to see if it is bubbling away. At first, if you peek too early, it may look as if it has solidified. However, if you let it simmer over low heat for a couple of more minutes, it will start to liquefy again and bubble away. When the agar is fully dissolved, pour in the cultured cashew mixture. Whisk quickly. While the mixture heats, dissolve the tapioca in the remaining 2 tablespoons water and add to the mixture. Continue cooking until the mixture is stretchy and shiny. Mix in the jalapeños and pour into a glass or metal container, preferably square or rectangular. Refrigerate until set, at least 4 hours. Wrap the cheese in wax paper and store it in the refrigerator for 2 to 3 weeks.

MAKES ABOUT 1 POUND

easy rejuvelac

Fear not—making rejuvelac is really not that complicated or scary.

½ cup quinoa or wheat berries

Put the quinoa or wheat berries into a 1-quart wide-mouth jar. (Make sure that the grains aren't already presprouted!). Cover them with water and let sit for 8 to 12 hours, then drain. Secure the top with cheesecloth and rinse and drain the grains twice a day until you see sprouts—quinoa sprouts in less than 24 hours, whereas wheat berries generally take about 2 days. Now fill the jar with filtered water, cover with a lid, and leave at room temperature (out of direct sunlight) for 2 to 3 days, until the water is cloudy and bubbly. Strain out the seeds and refrigerate the liquid, which is now lactic acid–rich rejuvelac. You can turn the strained sprouts into another batch of rejuvelac by filling the jar with water and letting it sit for another couple of days. The rejuvelac keeps in the refrigerator for 3 to 4 weeks.

MAKES ABOUT 4 CUPS

oil-free melty "mozzarella"

This mozzarella alternative is a great oil-free option for your pizza and panini!

1 cup cashews

1 cup Easy Rejuvelac (page 71) or juice from sauerkraut

1½ teaspoons sea salt

1 teaspoon nutritional yeast

1 teaspoon white, yellow, or chickpea miso

½ teaspoon onion powder

½ cup plus 2 tablespoons water

1 tablespoon agar powder

2 tablespoons tapioca

Place the cashews, rejuvelac, salt, nutritional yeast, miso, and onion powder in a blender and puree until smooth. Transfer to a clean container or jar, cover with a lid, and let sit at room temperature for 1 or 2 days, until the mixture has thickened, risen, and formed air pockets and is tangy. The texture will also have changed, and it will be somewhat gooey and thick.

Put the ½ cup water in a small saucepan with the agar powder and whisk well. Cover the pot with a lid and bring to a simmer over low heat. Don't peek for 3 to 4 minutes, then check to see if it is bubbling away. At first, if you peek too early, it may look as if it has solidified. However, if you let it simmer over low heat for a couple of minutes more, it will start to liquefy again and bubble away. When the agar is fully dissolved, pour in the cultured cashew mixture. Whisk quickly. While the mixture heats, dissolve the tapioca in the remaining 2 tablespoons water and add to the mixture. Continue cooking until the mixture is stretchy and shiny. Pour into a glass container of choice. Refrigerate until set, at least 4 hours. Wrap the cheese in wax paper and store it in the refrigerator for 2 to 3 weeks.

MAKES ABOUT 1 POUND

oil-free melty "cheddar"

Whether it's mac and cheese you're craving or just a great grilled cheese
sandwich, look no further than this oil-free, whole food, vegan answer
to Cheddar!

1 cup cashews

1 cup Easy Rejuvelac (page 71) or juice
from sauerkraut

1 teaspoon sea salt

3 tablespoons nutritional yeast

2 tablespoons white, yellow,
or chickpea miso

½ cup plus 2 tablespoons water

1 tablespoon agar powder

2 tablespoons tapioca

Place the cashews, rejuvelac, salt, nutritional yeast, and miso in a blender and puree
until smooth. Pour into a clean container or jar, cover with a lid, and let sit at room
temperature for 1 or 2 days, until the mixture has thickened, risen, and formed air
pockets and is tangy.

Put the ½ cup water in a small saucepan with the agar powder. Whisk to combine.
Cover the pot with a lid and bring to a simmer over low heat. Don't peek for 3 to
4 minutes, then check to see if it is bubbling away. At first, if you peek too early, it
may look as if it has solidified. However, if you let it simmer over low heat for a couple
of minutes more, it will start to liquefy again and bubble away. When the agar is
fully dissolved, pour in the cultured mixture. Whisk quickly. While the mixture heats,
dissolve the tapioca in the remaining 2 tablespoons water, and add to the mixture.
Continue cooking until the mixture is stretchy and shiny. Pour into a glass container
of choice. Refrigerate until set, at least 4 hours. Wrap the cheese in wax paper and
store it in the refrigerator for 2 to 3 weeks.

MAKES ABOUT 1 POUND

almond "feta"

I had almost forgotten the joy that feta cheese can add to dishes. For example, the wonderful Greek spinach pie, spanakopita—I had basically given up on this entirely. I'd made and had many vegan versions of it, but without the briny flavor of feta, the flavors just fell flat. After much knocking around in my noggin, I came up with the perfect vegan substitute. Salty and briny, this feta works beautifully crumbled over salads or slightly melted in all of the traditional dishes. Best of all, stored in brine, it keeps for weeks, getting stronger in flavor and more delicious as time goes by (in fact, it vastly improves after a month, so make this weeks ahead of time if you can).

---

2 cups blanched almonds, soaked in water for 12 to 24 hours

1 cup Easy Rejuvelac (page 71) or juice from sauerkraut

½ teaspoon sea salt

⅔ cup water

2 tablespoons agar powder

BRINE

6 cups water

¾ cup sea salt or kosher salt

Drain and rinse the almonds. Place them in a high-speed blender with the rejuvelac and salt, and process on the highest setting for 1 to 2 minutes until smooth and no longer grainy to the tongue. Pour the mixture into a clean container and cover with a nonpermeable lid or plastic wrap. Leave on your kitchen counter for 1 to 2 days to culture, making sure you taste it each day, until it begins to get tangy. Keep in mind there is no hard and fast rule about how long it needs to culture—your taste buds will have to guide you in determining the right length of time. In warmer weather, it could be just a day, while in cooler weather, it could take 2 days or even longer.

Once the cheese is slightly tangy, you can move onto solidifying it. First, prepare the mold for the cheese by lining an 8-inch square pan with cheesecloth. Combine the water and agar in a medium saucepan and whisk well. Cover the pan with a lid and bring to a simmer over low heat. Don't peek for 3 to 4 minutes, then check to see if it is bubbling away. At first, if you peek too early, it may look as if it has solidified. However, if you let it simmer over low heat for a couple of minutes more, it will start to liquefy again and bubble away. When the agar is fully dissolved, pour in the

continued >

◁ almond "feta," continued

cultured almond mixture and whisk immediately until fully combined. Pour the cheese mixture into the cheesecloth-lined pan. Refrigerate for several hours, until hard.

Prepare the brine by whisking together the water and the salt in a large bowl until most of the salt is dissolved. Cut the cheese into four pieces and place in the brine. Cover and let sit for 8 hours at room temperature. Transfer the cheese to a storage container and pour the brine over the cheese until it is halfway submerged. Add more plain water to completely cover the cheese and dilute the brine. Store in the refrigerator for up to 3 or 4 months. The flavor vastly improves after the first 3 to 4 weeks.

MAKES 1 POUND

vegan shaved "parmesan"

Big, flaky shards of sharp Parmesan to toss with Caesar salad, sprinkle on pasta, or melt on garlic bread is what this is all about. It's cultured, so get a 2- to 3-day head start if you're planning a big Italian feast for the weekend.

1 cup Brazil nuts, soaked in water for at least 4 hours

½ cup pine nuts

½ cup Easy Rejuvelac (page 71) or juice from sauerkraut

2 tablespoons white, yellow, or chickpea miso

¼ cup nutritional yeast

1 teaspoon sea salt

Drain the Brazil nuts and place with all of the other ingredients in a blender or food processor (a high-speed blender will create the smoothest texture, but I've made this in a food processor as well). Puree at the highest setting until the mixture is smooth, about 1 to 2 minutes. Put it in a covered container and set aside at room temperature for 2 to 3 days, until the flavors are nice and sharp and have deepened.

Preheat the oven to 250°F. Line two half-sheet pans or baking sheets with parchment paper or nonstick silicone baking liners. Using a cake decorating spatula or other flat device, spread the mixture almost paper-thin on the sheet pans. Depending on the size of your pans, you may need up to three. Bake for about 30 minutes, rotating the sheets after 15 minutes if your oven has hot spots or bakes unevenly, until dry and golden brown. Let it cool, then break into shards. Stored in a glass container, Vegan Shaved "Parmesan" will keep for 3 to 4 months in the refrigerator.

MAKES ABOUT 2 CUPS

not nog

A holiday favorite for years, this is what I serve unabashedly to everyone who walks through my door at that time of year. No one misses the eggs. Thick, creamy, and rich, it's delicious either plain or spiked. And if there's any left over, sweeten it a bit more and throw it into your ice cream maker for a delicious frozen dessert!

4 cups homemade soy milk (page 51) or almond milk (page 54) or store-bought variety

½ to ¾ cup maple syrup

½ cup cashews

1 tablespoon vanilla extract

½ teaspoon ground nutmeg, or more if you like

½ cup brandy or rum (optional)

Place the milk, ½ cup maple syrup (or more, depending on how sweet you like it), cashews, and vanilla in a blender and process until frothy and smooth. Add the nutmeg. Mix in the alcohol and chill for several hours before serving. Top each glass with an additional grating of nutmeg. Not Nog is best if consumed within 3 to 4 days. Be sure to keep it refrigerated!

MAKES ABOUT 5 CUPS

better than whipping cream and topping

This fluffy, light-as-air whipped cream is perfect for topping pies, berries, and sundaes, not to mention Sunday-morning waffles and blintzes. Make ahead and keep some on hand in the freezer to whip up whenever the mood strikes. Using soy milk will mimic whipped cream, while water (see Variation) will make it similar to Cool Whip. Take your pick and make a grand dessert!

1 cup homemade soy milk (page 51) or store-bought variety

½ cup refined coconut oil, melted

¼ cup cashews

¼ to ⅓ cup organic sugar

1 teaspoon vanilla extract

Place all of the ingredients in a blender and puree until smooth. You can use more or less sugar, depending on how sweet you like it. Pour into a covered container and refrigerate overnight or partially freeze for 2 to 3 hours or longer. Whip using an electric mixer until soft peaks form, 5 to 8 minutes. The mixture can become quite stiff if you continue whipping but can separate if overwhipped, so exercise caution. Keep the cream in a jar in the refrigerator for up to 1 week or in the freezer for up to 6 months.

Note: The colder the cream, the easier and quicker it will whip. If the cream doesn't begin to thicken after 5 to 6 minutes, freeze for an hour or so. Using a chilled bowl is also helpful. Also, the more sugar, the easier it may whip.

MAKES 2 CUPS WHIPPED CREAM OR TOPPING (RECIPE MAY BE DOUBLED)

VARIATION

COOL WHIP–STYLE WHIPPED CREAM Use water instead of soy milk and add 1 teaspoon guar or xanthan gum to the mixture.

all you need is soup

Soups are both a convenience food and a staple in my house. But a tasty soup always starts with a good stock. In this chapter, I'll show you how to make four distinct stocks from scratch, as well as your own flavorful bouillon for the times when you just want to be able to reach into your cupboard and turn water into stock.

Do you have a French onion soup recipe requiring a beef stock? Try the Got No Beef Broth (page 83). Or a delicate vichyssoise needing a rich but flavorful faux chicken broth? Try the Truly Free-Range Chicken(less) Stock (page 82). How about those hard-to-capture flavors of the sea? There's a Rich See-Food Stock (page 84). And finally, Mushroom Stock (page 85) adds incomparable woodsy flavor and depth to risottos, pastas, sauces, and of course, mushroom soup.

For good measure, I've added recipes for some great soups that will reward you for taking the time to make these flavorful stocks. But in case you're really looking for convenience, you'll find a few "almost-instant" concentrated soups. Instant soup concentrates are my answer to Campbell's. These are quickly made condensed soups that can be packed in jars or baggies, refrigerated or frozen, then reconstituted with some water or nondairy milk to make just a cup or two or more to go with a sandwich for a quick lunch or as an afternoon snack for the kids. And they're made from all fresh ingredients, so they taste much better than the canned versions. Instead of flour or cornstarch, I use whole rice and cashews to create a silky, creamy texture. Here, I present three flavors of concentrates based on traditional varieties—tomato (page 90), mushroom (page 91), and broccoli (page 92). The flavors are different, but the method is similar for all.

truly free-range chicken(less) stock

This light-colored, neutral stock with rich flavor is perfect for almost every application.

---

2 tablespoons oil (optional)

2 onions

8 ounces carrots

1 pound celery

1 pound potatoes

8 ounces sweet potatoes

4 ounces mushrooms

12 cups water

2 tablespoons nutritional yeast

2 to 3 teaspoons sea salt

1 teaspoon poultry seasoning, or a mixture of 1 teaspoon rubbed sage, ½ teaspoon dried thyme, and ½ teaspoon dried marjoram

Chop, dice, slice, or cut the veggies any way you want, as long as they are all relatively similar in size. Except for the onions, you needn't peel the vegetables. Whether or not you use oil to sauté the vegetables first is also up to you—the oil makes it a little richer, like chicken stock, which gets part of its flavor from the fat. But you can skip the sautéing step and simply simmer everything to make it oil-free. If you're using the oil, heat it in a large stockpot over medium heat, then sauté the onions, carrots, and celery in it for about 5 minutes to soften slightly. Otherwise, just throw them into the pot and follow the remaining steps.

Add both kinds of potatoes, mushrooms, water, nutritional yeast, salt, and poultry seasoning. Cover the pot, bring it to a boil over high heat, then lower the heat to medium-low and simmer for about 1 hour. The stock should be golden in color and richly flavored. Adjust the seasoning to your liking, then strain through a sieve (reserve the veggies for Curried Cream of Vegetable Soup, below). Store in an airtight container in the fridge for 3 to 4 days or in the freezer for up to 6 months.

MAKES 8 CUPS

> **BONUS RECIPE**
>
> CURRIED CREAM OF VEGETABLE SOUP Wait! Don't throw away the strained veggies! Make a bonus soup—puree them in a blender with an equal amount of water and/or cashew milk and season with a little curry powder and salt and pepper. Voilà!

got no beef broth

This rich broth gets deep, dark color and flavor from the long caramelization of the bouquet garni at the beginning. It can seem a little fussy, but you just need to hang around the kitchen enough to check on the process every few minutes and give it a stir. It certainly has the requisite umami of beef stock and stands in beautifully for it. As a bonus, the strained veggies from this can be used to make the best homemade veggie dogs!

---

1 pound onions, diced

12 ounces celery, diced

8 ounces carrots, diced

Sea salt

8 cups water

4 ounces mushrooms, sliced

¼ cup dried porcini mushrooms or shiitakes

¼ cup soy sauce

1 tablespoon red miso

1 tablespoon balsamic vinegar

6 cloves garlic

Heat a large heavy stockpot over high heat. No oil is necessary. Add the onions, celery, and carrots and sprinkle with a generous pinch of salt. Now, you're going to spend 30 to 40 minutes caramelizing the vegetables, letting them sweeten and brown without burning them. Sauté the vegetables over high heat to prevent them from getting too watery (if the veggies start to burn, turn down the heat as necessary). As the vegetables soften and become drier, turn the heat down. It's okay if they start to stick to the pan; you actually want to encourage that without burning. When they start to stick to the pan, sprinkle them with just a little bit of water, a tablespoon or so, just to loosen them and then scrape them with a wooden spoon. You don't need to stir the whole time, as the vegetables need to be left alone for minutes at a time in order to brown. Keep the heat at a level where they will stick a bit and get brown, but not burn. Keep doing this for a while, until they are quite reduced and nicely browned; the bottom of the pan will have stuff stuck to it as well.

Now add the 8 cups water, which will deglaze the pan and lift everything off. Add the mushrooms, soy sauce, miso, vinegar, and garlic. Cover the pot and bring to a boil over high heat, then turn it down and simmer for 30 minutes. Strain through a sieve, pushing the juices out of the vegetables. Reserve the vegetables and use to make Veggie Dogs (page 120). Store in an airtight container in the fridge for 3 to 4 days or in the freezer for up to 6 months.

MAKES 8 CUPS

rich see-food stock

This full-flavored version of Easy See-Food Stock (see Variation, below) provides the perfect backbone for bouillabaisse and cioppino (page 93).

2 tablespoons extra-virgin olive oil

1 onion, sliced

1 leek, sliced

3 medium carrots, sliced

3 cloves garlic, sliced

8 cups water

1 cup white wine

4 by 4-inch piece of konbu

1 teaspoon sea salt

10 to 12 peppercorns

½ cup firmly packed dulse (if available, use smoked dulse)

Heat the oil in a stockpot over medium heat. Add the vegetables and garlic and sauté for several minutes to wilt. Add the water, wine, konbu, salt, and peppercorns. Bring to a boil, turn down the heat, and simmer for about 45 minutes. Add the dulse and simmer for another minute, then remove from the heat. Let it sit for 15 minutes, then strain through a sieve. Store in an airtight container in the fridge for 3 to 4 days or in the freezer for up to 6 months.

MAKES 6 CUPS

VARIATION

EASY SEE-FOOD STOCK For a faster, less fishy version, decrease the water to 6 cups and omit all other ingredients except the konbu, salt, and dulse. Place the water, kombu, and salt in a 2-quart pot over medium heat and bring to a boil. Add the dulse and simmer for 1 minute. Remove from the heat and let sit for 1 hour. Strain through a sieve.

mushroom stock

This earthy stock adds incomparable umami and depth to all sorts of dishes beyond just soup. Try it in the Farro Risotto with Mushroom Medley (recipe follows), whip up a delicious stroganoff, or make a velvety mushroom sauce for tofu or seitan.

1 ounce dried porcini mushrooms

2 cups hot water

1 tablespoon oil or water

2 medium onions, or 1½ large onions, sliced or diced

2 carrots, sliced or diced

4 cups sliced white or cremini mushrooms

8 cups water

¾ cup red wine

1 cup dried shiitakes

1 teaspoon sea salt

2 sprigs fresh thyme

Soak the porcini mushrooms in the hot water in a small bowl for about 20 minutes. Meanwhile, heat the oil in a large stockpot over medium heat. Add the onions and carrots, cover, and sauté for about 5 minutes, until wilted. Add the sliced mushrooms and sauté again until wilted.

Add the water, along with the wine, dried shiitakes, salt, and porcini mushrooms with soaking liquid, taking care not to add the last tablespoon or so of liquid, which can contain sediment. Cover with a lid and simmer for 1 hour. Add the thyme and simmer for another 5 minutes.

Check the flavor: if too weak, remove the lid and boil down rapidly to concentrate the flavor. Strain into a bowl through a sieve, pressing the juices out (reserve the veggies to make Mushroom Pâté, page 87). Store in an airtight container in the fridge for 3 to 4 days or in the freezer for up to 6 months.

MAKES 6 TO 8 CUPS, DEPENDING ON DESIRED STRENGTH

continued ⌒

HOW TO USE MUSHROOM STOCK

farro risotto with mushroom medley

Farro, with its chewy texture, is reminiscent of barley but with a more refined flavor. I love it cooked on its own in place of rice, or in salads and soups. But my favorite way of serving it is as risotto, especially when combined with the earthiness of mushrooms. This recipe features both fresh and dried mushrooms, and the fresh ones are roasted separately in a wine bath, infusing them with wonderful flavor. I frequently teach this dish, and students always marvel at how easily it comes together, while yielding such rich, deep, complex flavors. Like the Roasted Tomato Risotto (page 35), this, too, is made almost entirely in the oven, freeing you up from slaving away at the stove. It is delicious when made entirely oil-free, or a bit of olive oil can be added to the mushrooms for enhanced richness and succulence.

¼ cup dried porcini mushrooms

1 cup hot water

1 large onion, diced

2 cloves garlic, minced

5 cups Mushroom Stock (page 85), plus more for sautéing

1½ cups farro

Sea salt

1 tablespoon chopped fresh thyme

1 tablespoon chopped fresh rosemary

Freshly ground black pepper

ROASTED MUSHROOM MEDLEY

6 to 8 cups sliced mushrooms, such as shiitakes, morels, chanterelles, cremini, button, portobello, oyster, king trumpet (a variety works best)

½ cup dry red wine, or ¼ cup dry sherry

3 tablespoons soy sauce

3 tablespoons olive oil (optional)

1 tablespoon mirin (sweet sake; see sidebar, page 27)

2 cloves garlic, minced

Soak the porcini mushrooms in the hot water in a small bowl for about 20 minutes.

To make the mushroom medley, preheat the oven to 350°F. Put all of the mushroom medley ingredients in a shallow baking dish and roast for about 30 minutes, until most of the liquid has been absorbed and the mushrooms are shrunken and dark.

Meanwhile, heat a heavy ovenproof pot or Dutch oven over medium heat. Add the onion and garlic and sauté, dry, until the onion begins to brown and stick. Pour in a tablespoon or two of stock to deglaze the pot, and continue to sauté until tender (or you can sauté in olive oil if desired). Add the farro and the 5 cups of stock, cover with a lid, and place in the oven. Bake for about 20 minutes (this can be baked alongside the mushroom medley). Remove from the oven momentarily to add the cooked mushrooms and soaked porcinis with their soaking liquid and have a taste to see if additional salt is necessary. If so, season with salt, then cover and return to the oven. Cook for another 10 minutes or so, then stir in the thyme and rosemary. Taste the farro—if it is al dente tender, it is ready to serve. If not, put it back in the oven and cook for a few more minutes. Grind some fresh black pepper on top before serving.

MAKES 6 TO 8 SERVINGS

BONUS RECIPE

MUSHROOM PÂTÉ Wait! Don't discard the strained veggies from the mushroom stock! Use them to make a quick mushroom pâté. Put the veggies in a food processor with ½ cup toasted walnuts, 1 cup chopped parsley, 2 or 3 cloves garlic, a pinch of ground allspice, some fresh or dried thyme, and sea salt and freshly ground black pepper to taste. Pulse until it reaches a desired consistency—it can be slightly chunky or smooth. Serve with crackers or bread or use it as a sandwich filling. Store in an airtight container in the fridge for up to 1 week. Freezing is not recommended, as it changes the texture.

brilliant bouillon

There's no substitute for a slowly simmered homemade stock for adding extra oomph to soups and sauces, but sometimes there's no time for that—not even in my household, where I pride myself on making just about everything from scratch. One time, when I ran out of my favorite organic veggie bouillon, I concocted my own. Whipped up in just a couple of minutes, it is truly instant—instant to make, and instant to use! And it's much cheaper, more flavorful, and less salty than the packaged variety, yielding a soothing cup of warm broth that's tasty enough to drink on its own or with just a couple of veggies thrown in. Make a jar of this and keep it in your cupboard. You'll find endless uses for it, from soups and sauces to adding a little extra flavor to casseroles, stir-fries, grains, and beans.

½ cup nutritional yeast

¼ cup porcini mushroom powder, or 6 tablespoons shiitake powder (recipe follows)

¼ cup white miso

¼ cup canola or other neutral oil

3 tablespoons soy sauce

1 tablespoon onion powder

1 tablespoon garlic powder

1 tablespoon ground celery seed

2 teaspoons sea salt

Combine all of the ingredients in a bowl and mix with a wooden spoon or process in a food processor to form a paste. Store this in a jar. In the pantry, it will keep for 4 to 6 weeks; in the refrigerator, for 3 to 4 months.

MAKES ⅔ CUP, ENOUGH FOR 16 TO 20 CUPS BROTH

mushroom powder

For all but the Chickenless Bouillon (see Variations, below), I prefer porcini mushrooms, but shiitakes are less expensive and more widely available.

1 ounce dried porcini mushrooms or shiitakes

Simply process the dried mushrooms in a blender until powdered. Store it in a jar in the cupboard for up to 6 months (or until the "use by" date on the package of the mushrooms you used) and add to soups, sauces, or beans to add a bit of umami and flavor.

MAKES 1 OUNCE

VARIATIONS

TOMATO-FLAVORED BOUILLON This is good for minestrone and other soups where a hint of tomato is desired. Make the soup base above in the food processor. Add ½ cup of sun-dried tomatoes, either reconstituted, oil-packed, or dried ones that are soft enough not to require soaking, if you can find them. Process until a relatively smooth paste is formed.

CHICKENLESS BOUILLON Increase the nutritional yeast by 2 tablespoons, use shiitake powder instead of porcini, and add 1 tablespoon poultry seasoning.

tomato soup concentrate

Back in the good old days, soup meant opening up a can and adding some milk or water. While big pots of fresh ingredients will always surpass instant, it's nice to have a fallback measure. This, and the two soups that follow, are my answers to instant soup. They are quickly prepared and can be packed in jars or baggies, refrigerated or frozen, then reconstituted with water or nondairy milk whenever you want.

This is full of good tomato flavor and can be enjoyed as soup, or in its concentrated form, as a sauce for pasta or casseroles.

Oil or water, for sautéing

1 medium onion, finely diced

½ cup thinly sliced celery

1½ pounds fresh tomatoes, diced

1½ cups water

¼ cup white rice

¼ cup cashews (optional)

2 tablespoons Brilliant Bouillon (page 88), 3 vegetable bouillon cubes, or 1 tablespoon powdered vegetable stock (or enough for 3 cups water)

¼ cup tomato paste

Sea salt and freshly ground black pepper

In a medium saucepan over medium-low heat, add a little oil or water and sauté the onion and celery until tender. Add the tomatoes, 1½ cups water, rice, cashews (to lend a creamier consistency), and bouillon, and bring to a boil over medium heat. Cover partially, turn the heat down to low, and simmer for about 15 minutes, until the rice is tender. Add the tomato paste and continue cooking for another 5 minutes, until the mixture is reduced by almost half and looks more like a thick sauce than a soup. Transfer the mixture to a blender or food processor, remove the cap in the lid to allow steam to escape, cover the hole with a kitchen towel, and puree until creamy or leave it slightly chunky. Season well with salt and pepper.

Let the mixture cool completely. Then pack it into jars, containers, or ziplock bags by the cup, or as you like. You can then refrigerate it for up to 1 week or keep it in the freezer for many months.

To reconstitute, put the container or bag in some hot water just long enough to melt the outside and let it slip out and into a pot. Add an equal amount of water or nondairy milk and heat until it has completely melted and the soup is hot.

MAKES 4 CUPS, ENOUGH FOR 8 CUPS SOUP

mushroom soup concentrate

A multiuse recipe, this makes a silky, rich soup base and, undiluted,
a great sauce for burgers, loaves, casseroles, and pastas.

Oil or water, for sautéing

1 medium onion, diced

3 stalks celery, diced

1½ pounds button or cremini mushrooms,
sliced

1 cup water

2 tablespoons Brilliant Bouillon (page 88),
3 vegetable bouillon cubes, or 1 tablespoon
powdered vegetable stock (or enough for
3 cups water)

1 teaspoon sea salt

¼ cup white rice

¼ cup cashews

2 tablespoons sherry (optional)

Freshly ground black pepper

In a medium saucepan over medium heat, add a little oil or water and sauté the
onion and celery until tender. Set aside 4 ounces of the mushrooms for later and
add the rest of them to the saucepan, along with the 1 cup water, bouillon, and salt.
Cover the pan and simmer for about 5 minutes, letting the juices come out of the
mushrooms. Add the rice, cashews, and sherry, cover again, and simmer for about
15 minutes, until the rice is tender and there is little liquid in the pot.

Let the mixture cool a bit, then puree in a blender until smooth (remove the cap
in the lid to allow steam to escape and cover the hole with a kitchen towel while
blending). Pour back into the pot. In another skillet over medium-high heat, sauté
the reserved mushrooms, either dry or in a bit of oil, then season them with a dash
of salt and pepper. Add the sautéed mushrooms to the soup mixture, give them
a stir, then let cool before packing it into jars, containers, or ziplock bags by the
cup, or as you like. You can then refrigerate it for up to 1 week or keep frozen for
many months.

To reconstitute, put the container or bag in some hot water just long enough to
melt the outside and let it slip out and into a pot. Add an equal amount of water
or nondairy milk and heat until it has completely melted and the soup is hot.

MAKES 4 CUPS, ENOUGH FOR 8 CUPS SOUP

cream of broccoli soup concentrate

This makes for an ultra-creamy, smooth, and comforting soup.

Oil or water, for sautéing

1 onion, diced

2 stalks celery, sliced

2½ cups water

½ cup white rice

½ cup cashews

2 tablespoons Brilliant Bouillon (page 88), 3 vegetable bouillon cubes, or 1 tablespoon powdered vegetable stock (or enough for 3 cups water)

1 teaspoon sea salt

1 head broccoli, or 1½ pounds broccoli florets

In a medium saucepan over medium heat, add a little oil or water and sauté the onion and celery until tender. Add the 2½ cups water, rice, cashews, bouillon, and salt. If you're using broccoli florets, add roughly half to the pot, reserving the rest for later. If you're using a whole head of broccoli, slice the stems thinly and toss them into the soup. Cut the tops up into small florets and set them aside.

Cover the pot, turn down the heat to low, and simmer for 15 to 20 minutes, until the rice is tender and there is minimal water left in the pot. Put the broccoli florets on top without stirring, cover the pot again, and steam for about 5 minutes, until the florets are tender (if you like, you can steam the florets in another pot, but why dirty one if you don't have to?). When the florets are very tender, remove them with a slotted spoon and set aside.

At this point, there should be very little liquid left in the pot. Let it cool a bit, then transfer the mixture to a blender and process until very smooth, silky, and creamy (remove the cap in the lid to allow steam to escape and cover the hole with a kitchen towel while blending). If the mixture is too thick and you have trouble blending, go ahead and add ¼ cup or so of water to help it process. Put the mixture back in the pot and stir in the steamed broccoli florets. You can now pack the soup in jars, containers, or by the cup in plastic ziplock bags for refrigerating or freezing. In the refrigerator, it will keep for about 1 week; in the freezer, it is best consumed within 3 months.

To reconstitute and heat the soup, for each 1 cup of soup concentrate, add ¾ cup water (not a full 1 cup as with the other soup recipes), because of the added florets.

MAKES 5 CUPS, ENOUGH FOR 8 CUPS SOUP

see-food cioppino

Cioppino, the American answer to bouillabaisse, hails from the wharves of San Francisco, where fishermen concocted a fragrant stew from the day's catch. The "day's catch" here is mushrooms, roasted until meaty and chewy. This soup gets better the longer it sits, so make it a day or two before you serve it.

---

2 pounds various mushrooms, such as oyster, lobster, king oyster, chanterelle, clamshell, shiitake

6 to 8 tablespoons extra-virgin olive oil

Sea salt and freshly ground black pepper

2 leeks, sliced

2 or 3 carrots, sliced

1 large fennel bulb, sliced

2 cups fennel stalks and fronds, if available, chopped

1 red bell pepper, cored, seeded, and diced

6 cups Rich See-Food Stock (page 84)

1 (28-ounce) can diced tomatoes

1 cup white or red wine

¼ cup tomato paste

1 head garlic, cloves sliced or minced

1 small red chile, finely sliced

2 bay leaves

1 teaspoon dried basil, or ¼ cup lightly packed fresh basil leaves

1 to 2 tablespoons Wakame Powder (page 29)

Preheat the oven to 425°F. Cut the mushrooms into large chunks. Spread them out in a single layer on two or three baking sheets and toss with a tablespoon or two of olive oil and season with salt and pepper. Roast them in the oven for 15 to 20 minutes, or until browned.

Meanwhile heat another 3 tablespoons of olive oil or water in a large, heavy pot. Add the leeks; carrots; fennel bulb, stalks, and fronds; and red bell pepper, and sauté over medium heat for 5 to 10 minutes, until tender. Now add the stock, tomatoes, wine, tomato paste, garlic, chile, bay leaves, and dried basil (if you're using fresh basil, don't add it now; wait until the end). Simmer for 30 to 40 minutes, until the flavors have melded and the soup looks luscious. Now add the roasted mushrooms and cook for an additional 5 minutes or so.

Finally, add the wakame powder, the fresh basil (if using), and another tablespoon or two of oil to really make it rich and flavorful. Keep the cioppino in an airtight container in the fridge for up to 5 days or in the freezer for up to 1 year—I did, and it was still delicious!

MAKES 6 TO 8 SERVINGS

see-food chowder

A big bowl of this comforting chowder speaks across generations, from kids to grandparents. You can make it as simple or as sophisticated as you like by varying (or not varying) the types of mushrooms you use.

2 pounds mixed mushrooms, including oyster, trumpet, chanterelle, straw, and shiitake

2 to 3 tablespoons olive oil

Sea salt and freshly ground black pepper

2 onions, diced

12 ounces waxy potatoes, diced

2 carrots, diced or sliced

1 red bell pepper, cored, seeded, and diced

5 cups Easy See-Food Stock (see Variation, page 84), Rich See-Food Stock (page 84), or Truly Free-Range Chicken(less) Stock (page 82)

3 cloves garlic, minced

1 tablespoon Wakame Powder (page 29)

1 cup cashews

2 cups water

½ cup minced parsley

Chunky bread, for serving

Preheat the oven to 425°F. Cut or tear the mushrooms into large bite-size pieces. Sprinkle with olive oil and season with salt and pepper. Spread onto baking sheets in one layer. Roast until browned and tender, about 20 minutes.

Meanwhile, in a heavy pot over medium heat, sauté the onions in a few tablespoons of water until soft. Add the potatoes, carrots, bell pepper, stock, garlic, and wakame powder and simmer until tender, about 20 minutes. Place the cashews and water in a blender and process until very smooth and creamy. Add the mushrooms to the soup, then add as much cashew cream as you like. Start with 1½ cups or so, then simmer for 1 minute to thicken slightly and add more if you like it creamier. Season with salt and pepper. Sprinkle with the parsley. Serve with chunky bread for soaking up the liquid. This chowder will keep in your fridge for 3 to 4 days.

MAKES 8 SERVINGS

curried butternut squash and coconut soup

I first had the combination of lemon and curry at an Indian restaurant in London and was immediately smitten. It's a dynamic combination where the verve of citrus complements the spicy sweetness of the soup, catapulting it from just yummy to spectacular. It's easy to make, too—just throw everything in the pot, simmer, and puree.

1 onion, sliced

7 cups cubed butternut squash, about 2½ pounds (peel and cut it yourself or just buy it already cut up!)

1 red bell pepper, cored, seeded, and sliced

1 celery stalk, sliced

4 cups Truly Free-Range Chicken(less) Stock (page 82)

1 to 2 tablespoons curry powder, depending on taste and curry powder used

7 ounces coconut milk (about half of a 13.5-ounce can)

1 to 2 teaspoons lemon zest

Sea salt and freshly ground black pepper

LEMON COCONUT CREAM
½ cup coconut milk

½ teaspoon lemon zest

1 to 2 tablespoons freshly squeezed lemon juice

¼ teaspoon sea salt

GARNISH (OPTIONAL)
½ cup slivered or sliced almonds, toasted

In a 2-quart saucepan over medium heat, combine the onion, squash, bell pepper, celery, stock, and curry powder, cover, and simmer until the vegetables are very tender. Using an immersion blender, process the mixture until smooth and creamy, or add the soup to a blender in batches to puree. To prevent the hot soup from splattering, remove the small cap from the lid to allow steam to escape, cover the hole with a kitchen towel, and blend until smooth and creamy; return to the saucepan. Stir in the coconut milk and lemon zest and season with salt and pepper.

To make the Lemon Coconut Cream, simply combine all of the ingredients in a small bowl and mix with a fork.

Pour the soup into individual bowls and top each bowl with a dollop of Lemon Coconut Cream and the toasted almonds. This soup is best enjoyed freshly made or the next day.

MAKES 8 SERVINGS

the meat of the argument

It's not just flesh that we call meat. Anything substantive, from the meat of coconut to the meat of the argument, can be referred to as that. So in this chapter, I use the term loosely, to describe foods with a bit of substance, stuff that has the chew factor. No matter what creative approaches we might take to construct our meals, the vast majority of people find comfort in a main dish that they can sink their teeth into. Hence, meat substitutes have become phenomenally huge in the marketplace. But they're expensive and often designed in the laboratory utilizing questionable ingredients, such as isolated soy protein. My first rule in cooking has always been to eat only what you can make in your kitchen. I once heard it described this way: if it comes from plants, eat it. If it's made in a plant, forget it.

My Japanese heritage has influenced me to harmonize as many elements as possible in a meal to balance flavors and derive optimal nutrition. In my household, we frequently go days or weeks without something "meaty" in the center of the plate, eating mostly veggies, legumes, and grains in myriad ways. But never to eat a succulent filet of UnSteak (page 127) with truffle sauce? Or tender-on-the-inside, crispy-on-the-outside nuggets (page 114)? Or crowd-pleasing Fab Cakes (page 109)? Come on, we don't have to be hardened legume eaters—there's room to enjoy both! From savory sausages to juicy UnRibs, kid-friendly nuggets to flaky fish fillet, you'll find it here. In addition, we'll explore a couple of the oldest foods on the planet, homemade fresh tofu and homemade tempeh, which, in my opinion, take the cake.

You might wonder why I suggest making quantities of the following recipes that look as if they might feed an army. The idea is not to cook something from scratch every day, but to have stuff on hand so you can make a quick meal when you want. So you'll end up with several pounds of UnSteak, or UnChicken, or UnPork, or a bunch of sausages. Tuck some away in the freezer for later, and meal creation will be a snap.

real tofu

Wait. Before you gloss over this recipe and chuckle, "Why would I want to make tofu?" just give me a chance to tell you why. First of all, it's super easy (really). It's also super fast. But for the real reason, read on.

Oh, I could wax poetic about tofu! Not the stuff sold in supermarkets—I can pass by most of that stuff. Freshly made tofu is a thing of beauty. It is subtly sweet, delicate, and yet full of depth. If I could just hand you a spoon now with a morsel of freshly made tofu, garnished with just a bit of ginger and a splash of soy sauce, I would need no words. You would go to your stove and make yourself a batch. Finally, you would understand the oft-misunderstood, oft-maligned, oft-mistreated white blocks. You would see that the real deal is something to be savored on its own, without having to be marinated, pureed, fried, baked, stewed, coated with bread crumbs, or in any other way have its true essence disguised.

And it gets better. There's a bit of science to it, but it's easy. It's just a matter of coagulating the soy milk and separating the curds from the whey (just like with cheese making). The curdling process takes just 2 to 3 minutes, and then you drain the curds. You can press or not press, depending on how firm you want your tofu. Pressing will yield a firmer texture, which is great for applications like grilling. You can add various seasonings at this point, such as herbs and garlic, sun-dried tomato and basil, and so on. The possibilities, as for many homemade things, are endless.

So I hope you won't pass this by. Just try it once, and I swear—your life will be forever changed.

For this recipe, you'll need a 6-inch sieve or colander and some cheesecloth. If you're pressing the tofu for a firm texture, you'll need a weight of some sort that fits into the sieve (such as a small glass container filled with water, a large rock, or a bag of beans) or a tofu press. Magnesium chloride (nigari) is available in some natural food stores or online.

---

4 cups plain soy milk, either homemade (page 51) or store-bought

½ teaspoon magnesium chloride (nigari)

¼ cup water

First, prepare your tofu mold—line a 6-inch sieve or colander with a double layer of cheesecloth and set it over a bowl or in the sink so the whey can drain and not get all over your counter. In a small bowl, mix the magnesium chloride and the water until dissolved and set aside.

If you make your own soy milk, the best time to make tofu is right after you've made it and it's still hot. But whether you're using freshly made soy milk or a store-bought variety, pour it into a 2-quart saucepan and bring it to a boil. Now add half to three-quarters of the magnesium chloride to the boiling soy milk and stir with a wooden spoon for 2 to 3 minutes while simmering over low heat. It should begin to curdle. If it doesn't separate into curds and whey, add the rest of the magnesium chloride water and stir again for 1 minute more.

Once it separates and the whey is clear (with a yellow tint, but no milkiness), pour the mixture through the sieve to collect the curds. Let it drain on its own for a few minutes until the mixture in the sieve has congealed and there is little water left. You can choose to press or not to press—that'll be the question. I like it Japanese-style, with a delicate texture, so I usually do not put a weight on it. But if you like it firmer, find an object in the kitchen to weight it down and make it more compact. Eat it right away or store in cool water in the refrigerator for 3 to 4 days.

MAKES 8 TO 12 OUNCES (RECIPE MAY BE DOUBLED)

VARIATIONS

VERY FIRM TOFU The more magnesium chloride, the firmer the tofu will be. Increase the magnesium chloride by 1/4 teaspoon. Press the curds with a weight to drain as much whey as possible.

FLAVORED TOFU After most of the whey has drained, add your favorite flavorings to the curds, mix lightly, then press. Garlic, herbs, lemon zest, sun-dried tomatoes, olives, capers, chiles, and salt and pepper can all put your unique stamp on your tofu.

fresh yuba (tofu skin)

What exactly is yuba, you might be thinking (I get this question a lot!). Simply put, it's the skin that forms on soy milk when it's heated, just like the skin that formed on milk when you made hot chocolate way back when. What can you do with it? For one, it forms the succulent, crispy skin that wraps around the "Breast" of UnChicken (page 112), and it makes a quick, easy bacon as well (page 103). You can also slice it into noodle-size strips and stir-fry with vegetables or add to soup. I am lucky enough to live in an area where I can buy it fresh, frozen, or dried, but I've included the recipe for those who live where it is not so readily available. Although it's easy enough to make, it requires hanging around the stove while your soy milk forms skins to be removed and dried—over and over again—so it's best to do when you have something else to be doing there as well.

**4 cups soy milk, either homemade
(page 51) or store-bought**

Pour the soy milk into a wide saucepan or deep skillet. The size of the skin will be the size of the pan you use, so choose your pot accordingly. For "Breast" of UnChicken, an 8-inch-diameter pot will be adequate, while a deep, 12-inch-diameter skillet will work for just about anything.

Turn the heat to medium and bring to just below a simmer—bubbles should be barely visible. After a couple of minutes, a skin will start to form. When the skin has formed all the way to the perimeter of the pan, take a sharp knife and run it along the edge to loosen it from the pan. Then insert a chopstick or dowel under the middle of the skin along the diameter and lift the skin off. Place on a baking sheet and unroll it so that it is open. Repeat this technique, stacking the yuba, until all of the milk has been used up.

To store the yuba, put it in a ziplock bag and refrigerate for several days or freeze for up to 1 year.

MAKES ABOUT 4 OUNCES

canadian yuba "bacon"

Tempeh bacon may be the rage, but in my opinion, it is too soft. When I want a BLT, I want not only flavor but also that crispy-on-the-outside, tender-on-the-inside texture. And yuba delivers. Make this, and everyone who walks into your kitchen and gets a big whiff of what you're cooking will think you abandoned the vegan ship.

8 ounces fresh or frozen yuba (page 102)

½ cup soy sauce or tamari

⅓ cup nutritional yeast

2 tablespoons maple syrup

½ to 1 teaspoon liquid smoke

Oil, for cooking

If you're using frozen yuba, let it thaw at room temperature, then soak in water for 3 to 5 minutes. Gently squeeze out as much water as possible and pat dry. If you're using fresh yuba, no preparation is necessary. Stack the yuba so that it is two or three layers thick. Cut it into strips about 1 inch wide. Some of the layers will come apart, but most of them will remain stuck together.

Combine the soy sauce, nutritional yeast, maple syrup, and liquid smoke in a medium bowl or shallow baking dish. Add the yuba strips and mix well. Marinate for a minimum of 30 minutes. Heat the oil in a skillet over medium heat. Remove the yuba pieces from the marinade and transfer the yuba to the skillet, frying on both sides until brown and crispy. Any leftover marinade can be stored in the refrigerator and used again. Store the yuba "bacon" in an airtight container in the fridge for 3 to 4 days or in the freezer for up to 6 months.

MAKES ABOUT 4 SERVINGS

VARIATIONS

OIL-FREE CANADIAN YUBA "BACON" Preheat the oven to 400°F. Spread the marinated strips on a nonstick baking sheet and bake for about 10 minutes, until browned.

tempeh

The first time I had tempeh was in the eighties at the sole Indonesian restaurant in Tokyo. It happened to be about two doors down from where I lived, so I went there often. I had my first durian there as well, and my first encounter with Japanese yakuza . . . but that's a tale better reserved for my memoirs.

Commercial tempeh has a distinct smell and taste that some people find off-putting. But freshly made tempeh has a delicate flavor accented by a nuanced nuttiness and faint mushroom aroma, and a pillowy soft texture. It's so good that even tempeh-haters often find themselves chowing down on it.

I am indebted to Philip Gelb, a local chef and friend, for providing me with a recipe with which I made my first batch. Phil is a kindred spirit who revels in making things from scratch—a man of my heart! The trickiest part of making tempeh is finding a way to replicate the climate of Indonesia—a temperature of around 85°F to 90°F—for 24 hours (see the end of the recipe for ideas). Start to finish, it'll take up to 48 hours, so don't plan on serving it tonight.

---

1 pound organic soybeans or chickpeas

1 tablespoons white vinegar

1 packet tempeh spores (amount will differ per manufacturer; see sidebar for sources)

Soak the soybeans in a large pot in plenty of water for 12 to 24 hours. You will now remove the hulls. To do so, rub the beans underwater between your hands to crack them. The hulls will rise to the surface of the water as you manipulate the soybeans, and you can get rid of them by using a small sieve to scoop them up (or tip the pot over and drain the water and hulls as the soybeans settle, a method that uses far more water). When all the hulls have been removed, drain the beans and refill the pot with fresh water.

Put the pot on the stove over high heat and bring the beans to a boil. Turn down the heat to medium low and simmer for 1 hour. Line an absolutely clean baking sheet (to prevent growth of unwanted pathogens) with several layers of paper towels. Drain the soybeans in a colander, then spread them out in a thin layer on the baking sheet to drain them further. Let them dry at room temperature for an hour or two. Moisture is the enemy of tempeh, so you want to make sure that the beans are really dry. If you have pets who hop on counters, I recommend covering the beans with paper towels as well.

When the beans are dry and at room temperature, put them in a large, clean bowl. Mix in the vinegar and the spores. Divide them between two quart-size ziplock bags and seal. Use a sterile skewer or needle (heat over a flame to sterilize) to poke holes into the bag every ¾ inch. The bags must be perforated in order for the spores to breathe. Too much humidity in the bags will cause spoilage and lead to the development of other unwanted molds.

You will now start the process of incubation, which can take 24 to 48 hours. Place the bags in an incubator (see sidebar) for 12 to 24 hours, until you see some white mycelium growing. The ideal temperature is 88°F, so if you can, try to be as close as possible during this period. When you see some white fuzz growing (the mycelium), there is enough self-generating heat in the tempeh that you can turn off your heat source and let it grow on its own. When the cakes are fully covered in white, put them in the refrigerator to stop any further growth; overdevelopment of the mycelium can lead to strong, bitter flavors.

The tempeh is now ready to use in your favorite recipes. Remember, tempeh is a living fungus and, as with all fungi, must be thoroughly cooked before ingesting in order for it to be fully digestible. Store in an airtight container in the fridge for up to 1 week or in the freezer for up to 6 months.

MAKES 1 POUND

TEMPEH TIPS AND RECOMMENDED EQUIPMENT

While tempeh spores will grow between 80°F to 91°F, the ideal temperature is 88°F. The spores can die above 92°F, so exercise caution. There are various potential methods for incubation. Before you start, I highly advise procuring a thermometer to check the ambient temperature of your incubator. If you have a dehydrator that has a low enough setting, you can use that. My oven has a setting of 100°F, but I found that the bottom shelf was actually 85°F, so I was able to incubate the tempeh there. Other people find that keeping the oven light on is adequate to raise the temperature to 80°F, the minimum required. Another method is to place a heating pad or warm bottles of water inside a Styrofoam cooler.

Tempeh spores can be ordered online at www.culturesforhealth.com, as well as www.organic-cultures.com and other sites.

flaky unfish

Being Japanese, I missed fish more than anything when I became vegan. After much experimenting, I found a way to create a flaky texture with just the right amount of fishiness—perfect for sole meunière or fish and chips or brushed lightly with teriyaki sauce.

Kelp powder is readily available in natural food stores.

8 ounces frozen yuba, or 12 ounces Fresh Yuba (page 102), plus 1 or 2 extra sheets (or 4 or 5 sheets nori) for wrapping

1 tablespoon soy sauce

1 tablespoon white or chickpea miso

1 tablespoon kelp powder

1 teaspoon Wakame Powder (page 29)

1 teaspoon sea salt

¾ cup water

4½ teaspoons agar powder

Preheat the oven to 400°F.

If you're using frozen yuba, let it thaw at room temperature, then rehydrate by soaking in water for 2 to 5 minutes. Squeeze it out to extract as much water as possible, then tear it roughly into 1-inch pieces and put it in the bowl of a food processor. If you're using fresh yuba, separate the sheets if they're stuck together, then tear them into approximately 1-inch pieces, and put them into the food processor. To the work bowl, add the soy sauce, miso, kelp powder (you can increase the quantity for a fishier flavor), Wakame Powder, and sea salt. Pulse the mixture until it resembles instant potato flakes, making sure you don't puree it smooth. Lightly packed, you should have about 4 cups.

Transfer the mixture to a medium bowl and mix in the water. Finally, sprinkle the agar powder over the mixture and mix well. Pat this into an 8 by 8-inch oiled baking dish. Cover well with aluminum foil and bake for an hour.

Because they contain agar, they will be very soft while hot but will congeal and become firm when cool. When they are firm, you can use them in any recipe calling for fish. Bread it and sauté, dip in beer or tempura batter and fry, or just sear and serve with Teriyaki Sauce (page 27) or lemon juice and capers. Store in an airtight container in the fridge for 3 to 4 days or in the freezer for up to 6 months.

MAKES 8 SERVINGS

unfish sticks

Okara again comes to the rescue, helping to create tender, flaky sticks.

1 pound regular, medium, or medium-firm tofu (do not use silken, firm, or extra firm)

1½ cups water

2 sheets nori, torn into small pieces

3 tablespoons nutritional yeast

2 tablespoons plus 1 teaspoon kelp powder (see recipe headnote, page 106)

1 tablespoon onion powder

2½ teaspoons sea salt

2 cups wheat gluten

2 cups okara (from making Creamy Soy Milk with No Beany Flavor, page 51)

½ cup all-purpose flour

3 tablespoons ground flax seeds

2 cups fine panko bread crumbs (see sidebar, page 128) or dry bread crumbs

Oil, for frying (optional)

Put the tofu, 1 cup of the water, the nori, the nutritional yeast, 2 tablespoons of the kelp powder, the onion powder, and 2 teaspoons of the salt in a food processor and process until creamy and smooth. Add the wheat gluten and pulse to mix well, then add the okara and pulse briefly until it is mixed evenly or mix by hand. The mixture should feel very light. Form the mixture into 30 fish sticks.

Create a three-dip coating station. Whisk together the following ingredients in each bowl.

Bowl 1: flour

Bowl 2: flax seeds and the remaining ½ cup water

Bowl 3: bread crumbs, the remaining 1 teaspoon kelp powder, and the remaining ½ teaspoon salt

You can bake or fry the fish sticks. To bake, preheat the oven to 350°F and line a baking sheet with parchment paper. Dip the fish sticks in the flour to coat, then the flax seed mixture, then the bread crumbs. Bake for 45 to 60 minutes, until slightly puffy and golden brown. To fry, put ¼ inch of oil in a skillet and heat over medium heat. When the oil is hot, put in the fish sticks, cover with a lid, and fry until golden brown on the bottom. Flip and cook the other side, until browned, 2 to 3 minutes on each side. Drain on paper towels. Store in an airtight container in the fridge for 3 to 4 days or in the freezer for up to 6 months.

MAKES ABOUT 30 STICKS

san francisco fab cakes with capers

When you make your own soy milk, you end up with a lot of pulp, which is called *okara* in Japanese. The Japanese make a dish of this by stewing it with vegetables and soy sauce, but most people here don't know what to do with it. Its flaky texture, however, is perfect for making your own vegan "crab" cakes. I tell you, they are just fab.

---

1 tablespoon olive oil or water

½ cup minced shallot

¼ cup minced red bell pepper

2 cups okara (from making Creamy Soy Milk with No Beany Flavor, page 51)

1 cup (about 6 ounces) mashed soft or silken tofu

½ cup Classic Eggless Mayonnaise (page 16) or Oil-Free Eggless Mayo (page 19)

½ cup minced parsley

2 tablespoons capers

1 tablespoon Dijon Mustard (page 21)

1 tablespoon Old Bay Seasoning

½ teaspoon smoked paprika

Sea salt and freshly ground black pepper

½ cup soft bread crumbs

3 sheets nori, torn into little pieces

About 1 cup panko bread crumbs (see sidebar, page 128)

Oil, for cooking

½ cup Wasabi Tartar Sauce, Wasabi Mayo, Chipotle Mayo, or Smoky Pimento Sauce (optional, recipes follow)

Heat the oil in a skillet and sauté the shallot and bell pepper until tender. Transfer to a large bowl and add the okara, tofu, mayonnaise, parsley, capers, mustard, Old Bay, and paprika and mix well. Season with salt and pepper. Mix in the soft bread crumbs and nori. Put the panko on a plate. Form the tofu mixture into little cakes 1½ to 2 inches in diameter and ⅓ to ½ inch thick, and dredge both sides in panko. Heat a tablespoon or two of oil in a large nonstick skillet over medium heat. Panfry the cakes on both sides until browned and crispy. Serve immediately, accompanied by one of the sauces.

MAKES 24 MINIATURE FAB CAKES OR 8 APPETIZER-SIZE FAB CAKES

continued ⌖

wasabi tartar sauce

Make this zesty spin on tartar sauce to serve with your
Fab Cakes. (Pictured on page 108.)

½ cup Classic Eggless Mayonnaise (page 16), Oil-Free Eggless Mayo
(page 19), or Lemon Cashew Mayo (page 18)

3 tablespoons chopped chives

2 tablespoons chopped green olives

2 tablespoons capers

1 tablespoon freshly squeezed lemon juice

1 to 3 teaspoons wasabi powder

Mix together all of the ingredients in a bowl and serve
with Fab Cakes. You can use more or less wasabi powder
depending on your desired heat level. Keeps for a week
in the refrigerator.

MAKES ⅔ CUP

wasabi mayo and chipotle mayo

If you want to keep it quick and simple, try these
suggestions for an instant sauce.

Into ½ cup of Classic Eggless Mayonnaise (page 16) or
Oil-Free Eggless Mayo (page 19), mix in up to 1 tablespoon
of wasabi powder for Wasabi Mayo, or 1 or 2 teaspoons of
chopped chipotle pepper in adobo sauce for Chipotle Mayo.

MAKES ½ CUP

smoky pimento sauce

This emphasizes the smoky hint in the Fab Cakes while complementing them with a rich sweetness.

1 red bell pepper

½ cup Classic Eggless Mayonnaise (page 16), Oil-Free Eggless Mayo (page 19), or Lemon Cashew Mayo (page 18)

1 teaspoon smoked paprika, either sweet or picante

Sea salt

Preheat the oven to 400°F. Put the bell pepper in a baking dish and cover with aluminum foil. Roast in the oven for about 30 minutes, until very soft and puffy. When it is cool enough to handle, remove the skins, stem, and seeds. Put the flesh in a food processor or blender with the mayonnaise and paprika and process until smooth, red, and creamy. Season with salt. Keeps in the refrigerator for 3 to 4 days.

MAKES ABOUT ⅔ CUP

"breast" of unchicken

No feather plucking necessary with these tender creatures, but you'll still get the same crispy skin. These beautiful "breasts" are easy to whip up and play nicely in everything from scaloppine to parmigiana to Chinese UnChicken salad to good ol' fried UnChicken. If you make them thin enough, you can even stuff them with some fancy rice filling, roll them up, sauce them, and impress all your guests. Make a good amount of this, enjoy some today, and then tuck the rest away in the freezer for another meal or two. They can be made with or without "skin."

FOR THE "BREASTS"

1 pound regular, medium, or medium-firm tofu (do not use silken, firm, or extra firm)

1 cup water

½ cup canola, safflower, sunflower, or other neutral oil or less (optional)

5 tablespoons nutritional yeast

2 tablespoons onion powder

4 teaspoons garlic powder

2 teaspoons poultry seasoning

2 teaspoons sea salt

3 to 3½ cups wheat gluten (reduce gluten by ¼ cup if oil is omitted)

Oil, for cooking

4 to 6 cups water

1 tablespoon soy sauce

FOR THE "SKIN" (OPTIONAL)

3 tablespoons oil

3 tablespoons white wine

2 tablespoons nutritional yeast

1 teaspoon poultry seasoning

½ teaspoon sea salt

2 sheets fresh, frozen, or dried Fresh Yuba (page 102) or store-bought yuba

To make the "breasts," put the tofu, water, oil (adds richer flavor), nutritional yeast, seasonings, and salt in a food processor and process until creamy and smooth. Add 3 cups of the wheat gluten and continue to process until a ball forms in the center. If you like your "meat" a little firmer, add an extra ½ cup of gluten. These are designed to be tender.

Put the mixture on a clean surface and roll it into a 3-inch-thick log. Slice the log into twelve slices. Now, pat each slice with the palm of your hand until it is 5 or 6 inches long and 3 inches wide.

Heat a little oil in a deep skillet or chef's pan (nonstick works well for this) and cook the patties over medium heat for 5 to 6 minutes on each side, until crispy and brown. If you have a really large skillet, you might be able to do this all at once; otherwise, sauté them in batches. When they are all nicely browned on both sides, put them all back in the pan (if you have cooked them in batches), and pour the water (add enough to cover the patties) and soy sauce over them. Cover the pan and simmer for about 30 minutes, until most of the water has been absorbed. Remove the "breasts" from the pan and let cool. They will seem quite soft but will firm up as they cool. At this point, they are "skinless" and can be used in vegan chicken salads or whatever else you prefer.

To dress them up with a succulent and crispy "skin," you will wrap up the breasts in seasoned sheets of yuba. First, preheat the oven to 375°F and line a baking sheet with parchment paper. Then, make the marinade by combining the oil, wine, nutritional yeast, seasoning, and salt in a bowl. Have a pastry brush ready to go. Now, depending on the type of yuba you're using, you may have to do a quick presoak. If you're using fresh yuba, you can skip this step. Otherwise, take your sheets of frozen or dry yuba and soak them in a pan of cold water for 2 to 10 minutes, until soft, pliable, and lighter in color. It's a good idea to work quickly, as oversoaking can make them fragile and difficult to handle (frozen yuba will be ready sooner than dry yuba). Take them out a sheet at a time and shake off the water. Cut or tear them into pieces large enough to wrap your "breasts" all around and wrap each piece completely. Brush them all over with the marinade and set on the baking sheet. Wrap and brush all of the pieces with yuba. If you need to do a patchwork of yuba to get a piece covered toward the end, that's fine. Bake them for about 30 minutes, until the yuba skin is crispy and golden brown. Store in an airtight container in the fridge for 3 to 4 days or in the freezer for up to 6 months.

MAKES 12 "BREASTS," OR ABOUT 4 POUNDS

gold nuggets or buffalo "wings"

Because these nuggets are so tender, they don't need a lot of oil (or any!) to be delicious. They're also an excellent use for any leftover okara from making soy milk, which makes an exceptionally flaky texture, or you can opt for the straight gluten version. How easy is dinner for the kids if you have some of these on hand in the freezer to heat up? I opt for the oil-free baked version, but if you have no fear of oil, go for the richer fried version.

1 pound soft, regular, medium, or medium-firm tofu (do not use firm or extra firm)

1 cup water

5 tablespoons nutritional yeast

2 tablespoons onion powder

4 teaspoons garlic powder

2 teaspoon poultry seasoning

2 teaspoons sea salt

2 cups vital wheat gluten

2 cups okara (from making Creamy Soy Milk with No Beany Flavor, page 51), or omit and increase vital wheat gluten to 2½ cups

FOR NUGGETS

½ cup all-purpose flour

1 tablespoon nutritional yeast

2 teaspoons poultry seasoning

2 teaspoons onion powder

1 teaspoon sea salt

3 tablespoons ground flax seeds

½ cup water

2 cups fine dry bread crumbs or panko bread crumbs (see sidebar, page 128)

1 teaspoon garlic powder

Oil, for frying (optional)

FOR BUFFALO "WINGS"

1½ cups buffalo wing sauce or Zippy Barbecue Sauce (page 30)

Ranch Dressing (page 39), for serving

Put the tofu, water, nutritional yeast, seasonings, and salt in a food processor and process until creamy and smooth. Add the wheat gluten and okara and continue to process until a ball forms in the center. Put the mixture on a clean surface and roll it into four 1-inch-thick logs. Slice each log into twelve slices. Now, pat each slice into a nugget or buffalo wing. Follow the steps below to make one or the other.

NUGGETS
Create a three-dip coating station. Whisk together the following ingredients in each bowl.

Bowl 1: flour, nutritional yeast, 1 teaspoon of the poultry seasoning, 1 teaspoon of the onion powder, and ½ teaspoon of the salt

Bowl 2: ground flax seeds and water

Bowl 3: bread crumbs, the remaining 1 teaspoon poultry seasoning, the remaining 1 teaspoon onion powder, the garlic powder, and the remaining ½ teaspoon salt

Dip the nuggets in the flour to coat, then the flax seed mixture, then the bread crumbs. You may now bake or fry the nuggets. To bake, preheat the oven to 350°F and line a baking sheet with parchment paper. Bake for 45 to 60 minutes, until slightly puffy and golden brown. To fry, put ¼ inch of oil in a skillet over medium heat. When the oil is hot, put in the nuggets, cover with a lid, and fry until golden brown on the bottom. Flip and cook the other side until browned, 2 to 3 minutes per side. Drain on paper towels. Store in an airtight container in the fridge for 3 to 4 days or in the freezer for up to 6 months.

BUFFALO "WINGS"
Preheat the oven to 350°F and line a baking sheet with parchment paper. Use your favorite buffalo wing sauce or barbecue sauce. After shaping the dough into wings, dip them in the sauce and place on the baking sheet, about 2 inches apart. Bake for 45 to 60 minutes, until slightly puffed and brown. Toss with a bit more of the sauce to refresh them and then serve with ranch dressing. Store in an airtight container in the fridge for 3 to 4 days or in the freezer for up to 6 months.

MAKES 4 DOZEN OR MORE

unpork

The technique for mixing this dough creates a stringy texture that is the perfect answer for pulled pork, pot stickers, dumplings, char siu pork, and pork buns. You can eat it as is or shred it, grind it, or marinate it. The liquid from cooking results in a rich broth full of depth and flavor, making it a perfect base for soups and my favorite, ramen.

1 cup water

⅓ cup oil

2 tablespoons organic sugar

1 tablespoon soy sauce

1 teaspoon liquid smoke

2 teaspoons onion powder

2 teaspoons sea salt

2¼ cups vital wheat gluten

Oil, for cooking

Mix the water, oil, sugar, soy sauce, liquid smoke, onion powder, and 1 teaspoon of the salt in a large bowl. Add about 2 cups of the vital wheat gluten and mix well. Finally, add the remaining ¼ cup gluten, working it in with your hands, breaking and stretching it until no dry flour shows. The dough will be rough and stringy (it's all in the mixing technique, so don't dump all the gluten in there at once!). Heat a deep skillet over medium heat with a little oil and cook the seitan pieces on both sides until browned. Cover with water, add the remaining 1 teaspoon salt, put a lid on the pan, and simmer for 30 minutes to 1 hour, until cooked through. You can check by cutting a piece in half; there should be tiny air pockets throughout. Use as desired and freeze the rest for later. Frozen, it will keep for 6 to 8 months.

Note: To increase the stringiness of the pork, decrease the initial amount of gluten added to 1¾ cups. After mixing well, add the remaining ½ cup. This will form smaller, stringier pieces.

MAKES 2¼ POUNDS

unribs

Here's another recipe that hearkens back to the days when I produced commercial meat substitutes. On the days we made UnRibs, you'd walk into the factory and get hit by the smoky smells of garlic, spice, tomatoes, and chiles wafting in the air. It would permeate my clothes, and I'd go home smelling like one giant rib. I'd grab several packages on my way out, and my kids would chomp on them right out of the bag. Ah, those were the days.

Recently, I found the old recipe. It starts out calling for 250 pounds of vital wheat gluten. Well, a few adjustments had to be made, of course. But over the years, I've had people ask me if I was ever going to include the UnRib recipe in a book . . . so here it is (almost). These are quite addictive, and I have to hide them from myself so I don't keep eating them. They really improve in flavor from sitting for a day or two, so make them ahead if you can. Then just keep them around for noshing.

To make it easier for folks, I've changed the technique slightly, giving you the option of making them low-fat or not. When I think of ribs, the words smoky, chewy, and savory certainly come to mind, but the word that tops it all is greasy. That flavorful grease dripping down your chin is one of the highlights, don't you think? Maybe not . . . so there's a version for you, too! Both versions are tasty, and I enjoy them both. Make a bunch, freeze them, and you can thaw, slice, and cook them whenever you want.

¼ cup soy sauce

3 tablespoons nutritional yeast

2 tablespoons smooth peanut butter

2 tablespoons tomato paste

1 tablespoon white, chickpea, or red miso

4 or 5 cloves garlic

1¼ cups water

2½ to 3 cups vital wheat gluten

Oil, for cooking (optional)

SAUCE

3½ to 4 cups Zippy Barbecue Sauce (page 30) or your favorite store-bought variety

2 cups water

continued ⟩

In a food processor or blender, combine the soy sauce, nutritional yeast, peanut butter, tomato paste, miso, garlic, and water and process until a smooth and creamy slurry is created. If you are using a food processor, just keep everything in there; if using a blender, pour it out into a large mixing bowl. Add 2½ cups of the gluten to the slurry and mix well, either using the food processor or by hand in the bowl. If you're using a food processor, keep pulsing to knead the dough, adding a little more gluten flour as necessary to form a stiff dough (the more gluten you add, the chewier your ribs will be, so you can control how tender or chewy you want them). It may form one ball in the center or break up into little beads; if the latter happens, all you have to do is push it together with your hands. If you're mixing it by hand, knead it in the bowl for several minutes until it becomes smooth.

Roll the dough into a log about 6 inches long. Slice the log lengthwise into four "steaks" about ¾ inch thick. Now here's one of the places where you get to decide whether or not to use oil, and how much. Heat a skillet over medium-low heat—if you're going for oil-free, make sure that it is nonstick. If you're using oil, add a couple of tablespoons to the skillet and let it get hot. Add the steaks and cook until browned on both sides. They will rise and puff a little.

Preheat the oven to 350°F. If your skillet is ovenproof, you can just leave the steaks in the pan. If not, transfer them to a baking dish. Mix 1½ cups of the barbecue sauce with the water. Pour the diluted sauce over the steaks in the pan and cover with a lid or aluminum foil. Bake the ribs for 75 to 90 minutes, until the sauce has reduced and just barely coats them and the steaks are chewy and cooked through. They will be relatively tender while hot but will deflate slightly and become chewier as they cool, so fear not if they seem too soft right out of the oven.

Let them cool until they can be handled without burning your fingers. Then slice each steak lengthwise into "ribs" about ⅓ to ½ inch thick. Heat the skillet over medium-low heat. You're going to sauté the individual ribs once more to brown or even blacken them on both sides. Once again, you can choose to oil or not to oil. If you like your ribs on the greasy side, you'll want to use a good 4 to 6 tablespoons of oil to sauté them. Or you can just use a dry nonstick skillet. Cook them all until nicely dark on both sides (I like them almost black). Then toss them with the remaining 2 to 2½ cups barbecue sauce. Now you can dig in. Or wait until the next day, when they will have deepened in flavor and become even chewier. To reheat, just throw them in the oven or on the grill, or eat them cold with some potato salad—yum! Store in an airtight container in the fridge for up to 1 week or in the freezer for up to 6 months.

MAKES 8 TO 10 SERVINGS

veggie dogs

Turn the leftover strained veggies from Got No Beef Broth (page 83) into fantastic veggie dogs or sausages!

Leftover veggies from Got No Beef Broth (page 83)

3 tablespoons tomato paste

3 tablespoons nutritional yeast

2 tablespoons soy sauce

1 tablespoon sea salt

2 teaspoons onion powder

2 teaspoons rice vinegar or apple cider vinegar

1 teaspoon liquid smoke

1 teaspoon smoked paprika

1 teaspoon organic sugar or maple syrup

3¼ cups vital wheat gluten

Hot dog buns and homemade condiments, for serving

Place the leftover veggies in a food processor and puree until smooth. Add the tomato paste, nutritional yeast, soy sauce, salt, onion powder, vinegar, liquid smoke, paprika, and sugar to the food processor and puree again until completely mixed. Finally, add the vital wheat gluten and process until thoroughly combined.

Form the mixture into ten to twelve wieners and wrap them well in aluminum foil. Stack them in a crisscross fashion in a steamer, leaving ½ inch between them, then steam for about 45 minutes, until they are firm and springy. Alternatively, bake in a preheated oven at 350°F for 1 hour (this method will form a slightly drier veggie dog). They will firm up as they cool. Then serve in buns with some homemade mustard! Store in an airtight container in the fridge for up to 1 week or in the freezer for up to 6 months.

MAKES 10 TO 12 VEGGIE DOGS

VARIATION

IMPROVISATIONAL UNSAUSAGES If you want sausages, omit the liquid smoke and add some sausage spices or Italian spice mixture instead. You can also bake this in a larger log (although it may take up to 2 hours) and make sliceable lunch meat. Play around with the seasonings—add cracked black pepper, fennel, sun-dried tomatoes, olives, whatever your imagination inspires—to make tasty variations.

italian unsausages

With bits of sun-dried tomatoes and garlic, these sausages will add pizzazz to pizzas and pasta.

½ cup bulgur wheat

1 cup boiling water

½ cup oil-packed or reconstituted sun-dried tomatoes, roughly chopped

¼ cup olive oil or water

2 cups diced onion

2 tablespoons minced fresh garlic

¼ cup water

¼ cup tomato paste

3 tablespoons soy sauce

2 tablespoons white or chickpea miso

2 tablespoons smooth peanut butter

1½ teaspoons fennel seeds

1½ teaspoons dried basil

1 teaspoon Sausage Spice (page 125)

½ teaspoon dried marjoram

½ teaspoon dried rosemary

½ teaspoon freshly ground black pepper

1½ cups vital wheat gluten

Put the bulgur wheat in a small heatproof bowl, pour the boiling water over it, cover, and let soak for 10 to 15 minutes. If you're using oil-packed sun-dried tomatoes, drain and rinse them under hot water to remove as much oil as possible.

Heat the oil in a medium saucepan over medium heat and sauté the onion and garlic until fairly tender (for an oil-free version, sauté them in a dry skillet, adding water as necessary to prevent sticking). Turn off the heat. Add the sun-dried tomatoes, water, tomato paste, soy sauce, miso, and peanut butter to the onions and garlic and mix well. Use an immersion blender or a food processor to roughly puree, making sure to leave some texture (don't puree it until smooth—you want some small bits of onion and sun-dried tomatoes). Put this slurry into a large mixing bowl.

Drain the bulgur. Add it to the slurry along with all of the spices. Now add the gluten and mix by hand to combine well. Roll the mixture into ten to twelve sausages 4 to 5 inches long and ¾ inch in diameter. Wrap each log tightly in aluminum foil. Place the logs in a steamer, leaving ½ inch between them, and steam for about 1 hour (if you need to stack them, crisscross them with space in between, to allow for steam circulation). They will be very soft at first but will firm up as they cool. Store in an airtight container in the fridge for up to 1 week or in the freezer for up to 6 months.

MAKES 10 TO 12 SAUSAGES

smoked apple and beer unsausages

A little bit sweet and savory, these are great off the grill and in a roll with some mustard (try the Ale and Brown Sugar Mustard, page 22, and pictured opposite), as well as sliced and tossed in your tofu scramble or bean soups.

½ cup bulgur wheat	2 tablespoons soy sauce
1 cup boiling water	2 tablespoons white or chickpea miso
¼ cup olive oil or water	1 tablespoon poultry seasoning
2 cups diced onion	1 tablespoon powdered sage
1 cup sliced mushrooms	2 teaspoons dried thyme
1 medium apple, cored and diced	½ teaspoon liquid smoke
½ cup beer or ale (I like an IPA)	⅛ teaspoon ground allspice
4 or 5 cloves garlic, sliced	1½ to 1¾ cups vital wheat gluten

Put the bulgur wheat in a small heatproof bowl, pour the boiling water over it, and cover with a lid or a plate. Let it soak for 10 to 15 minutes.

Heat the oil in a skillet or sauté pan over medium heat and sauté the onion until fairly tender. For an oil-free version, sauté the onion in a dry skillet, adding water as necessary to prevent sticking. Add the mushrooms and sauté until wilted. Transfer to a food processor or blender and add the apple, beer, 4 cloves garlic (or more, depending on how garlicky you like it), soy sauce, miso, poultry seasoning, sage, thyme, liquid smoke, and allspice. Pulse until it forms a slurry with a bit of texture; it does not need to be completely smooth. Put this slurry into a bowl.

Drain the bulgur and add it to the slurry. Mix in the wheat gluten—for a tender sausage, use just 1½ cups; for a firm one, use 1¾ cups. Roll the mixture into ten to twelve sausages 4 to 5 inches long and ¾ inch in diameter. Wrap each log tightly in aluminum foil. Place the logs in a steamer, leaving ½ inch between them, and steam for about 1 hour (if you need to stack them, do so in a crisscross manner with space in between, which will allow for better steam circulation). They will be very soft when they come out of the steamer but will firm up as they cool. Store in an airtight container in the fridge for up to 1 week or in the freezer for up to 6 months.

MAKES 10 TO 12 SAUSAGES

marvelous breakfast unsausages

If you've been craving a really tasty sausage for breakfast, look no further.
It's all in the spices, and these guys have it. I made my first sausages
in my early twenties, based on a recipe from Julia Child, swapping out
homemade gluten for the meat. Her spice mixture transformed tasteless
gluten into savory, zesty goodness. My take on her spice mixture is a
little more herb-forward, lending complexity and depth to these chewy,
juicy patties.

½ cup bulgur wheat

1 cup boiling water

¼ cup olive oil or water

2 cups diced onion

2 cups sliced mushrooms

4 or 5 cloves garlic, sliced

3 tablespoons soy sauce

2 tablespoons white or chickpea miso

½ cup water or broth

1 tablespoon Sausage Spice (recipe follows)

1½ to 1¾ cups vital wheat gluten

Add the bulgur wheat to a small heatproof bowl. Pour the boiling water over
the bulgur wheat and cover with a lid or plate. Let it soak while you prepare the
other ingredients.

Heat the oil in a large skillet and sauté the onion until fairly tender. For an oil-free
version, sauté the onion in a dry skillet, adding water as necessary to prevent
sticking. Add the mushrooms and sauté until wilted. Transfer to a food processor
or blender and add 4 cloves garlic (or more, depending on how garlicky you like it),
soy sauce, miso, water, and spice mixture. Pulse until a slurry with a bit of texture is
formed; it does not need to be completely smooth. Put this slurry into a large bowl.

Drain the bulgur and add it to the slurry. Mix in the wheat gluten to form a soft
dough. The more you use, the chewier it will be. Roll the mixture into two fat logs
about 2 inches in diameter and 7 to 8 inches long. Prepare two pieces of aluminum
foil about 2 inches wider and longer than the logs. Lightly oil the foil, then wrap
around the logs, closing the ends tightly. Place both logs in a steamer and steam
for about 1 hour. They will be very soft when they come out of the steamer but will
firm up as they cool. To serve, slice as desired and sauté on both sides. Store in an
airtight container in the fridge for up to 1 week or in the freezer for up to 6 months.

MAKES 6 TO 8 SERVINGS

sausage spice

Keep this on hand for not only sausages but also pot pies, stews, tofu, tempeh, and "meat" pies. You can easily double this if you like, since it seems to keep forever.

3 tablespoons rubbed sage (not ground)

1 tablespoon ground white pepper

1 tablespoon paprika

1 tablespoon dried thyme

1 teaspoon ground allspice

1 teaspoon ground nutmeg

1 teaspoon ground cinnamon

1 teaspoon ground cloves

1 teaspoon dried savory

Combine all of the spices in a jar and mix well.

MAKES ABOUT ½ CUP

peppy unpepperoni

My dear friend Camala Casco helped develop this flavorful pepperoni during the weekly testing parties I had at my house. She made it over and over again until it came out tasting just perfect. It's got that zing and is delicious in sandwiches, on pizza, or as part of a charcuterie board.

WET INGREDIENTS

½ cup red wine

¼ cup olive oil or nut butter of choice (peanut or walnut butter works great)

½ onion, roughly chopped

2 tablespoons red miso

1 tablespoon maple syrup

1 tablespoon soy sauce

1½ teaspoons liquid smoke

3 cloves garlic

DRY INGREDIENTS

1¾ cups vital wheat gluten

¼ cup nutritional yeast

1½ tablespoons Spanish smoked paprika

1½ teaspoons freshly ground black pepper

1½ teaspoons powdered mustard or freshly ground mustard seeds, either black or brown

1½ teaspoons ground fennel seeds

1½ teaspoons red pepper flakes

1 teaspoon sea salt

Preheat the oven to 325°F. Place all of the wet ingredients in a blender and puree until completely liquefied. Pour the mixture into a large bowl. In a separate medium bowl, mix together all of the dry ingredients, then add to the wet mixture and mix well.

Portion the dough into four equal pieces, then form each piece into a log approximately 1½ inches in diameter. Wrap each log in a double layer of oiled aluminum foil. Seal the ends well. Bake for 1 hour. Let cool completely before slicing. To slice, use a sharp knife, or refrigerate the logs overnight and then use the slicer attachment on a food processor. Store in an airtight container in the fridge for up to 1 week or in the freezer for up to 6 months.

Note: For pizza, toss the slices in a bit of olive oil to keep them from drying out.

MAKES 1 POUND

GRINDING SPICES

If you don't have ground spices, you can pulverize the mustard and fennel seeds in a little coffee grinder or do it manually with a mortar and pestle.

unsteak

Tender and juicy, UnSteak will prove to be a highly versatile and quintessential ingredient in your house for everything from steak sandwiches, to "veal Parmesan," to broccoli with "beef," to beef stew, to a rendition of your mom's meatloaf. Yes, it makes a lot, but you'll use it a lot. Slice it, grind it, cube it, sear it. You'll have it all covered with this. Keep in mind that you'll need a day to marinate the steak before using.

1 pound cremini or button mushrooms or shiitakes, roughly chopped (about 6 cups)

½ cup soy sauce

½ cup red wine

3 to 4 cloves garlic

2½ cups water or stock

5 to 5½ cups vital wheat gluten

MARINADE

2½ cups red wine

1¼ cup mirin (sweet sake; see sidebar, page 27)

1 cup soy sauce

1 head garlic, minced

Preheat the oven to 350°F and line two baking sheets with parchment paper. In a blender or food processor, combine the mushrooms, soy sauce, wine, and 3 cloves garlic (or more, depending on how garlicky you like it and the size of the cloves) and process until liquefied. Transfer to a bowl, then whisk in the water. With your hands or a wooden spoon, mix in 5 cups of the vital wheat gluten to form a very soft dough. If you have made seitan before, you may think that it is too soft, but don't worry! It's supposed to be really soft. However, if it seems really wet, or you prefer a slightly less tender seitan, mix in the remaining ½ cup gluten. Don't knead it, either—all you have to do is mix it up. Divide the dough into five pieces and shape each one roughly into a loaf like a French *bâtard* loaf. Space them at least 4 inches apart on the baking sheets and bake for 30 minutes, until puffy.

Meanwhile, bring a large pot of water to a boil (depending on the size of your pots, you may need two). Transfer the seitan loaves to the pot, partially cover with a lid, and simmer over medium-low heat for about 1 hour. Don't let it reach a fast boil, or the seitan could develop large air pockets—a low simmer is what you want. Let it cool down for a couple of hours before attempting to remove the loaves, as they will be very tender. Remove the seitan and cool completely before handling. The

continued >

cooking liquid can be used as a soup stock, so don't discard it! (You can refrigerate the liquid for use as stock for 3 to 4 days, or freeze for several months.)

While baking or simmering the seitan, make the marinade by simply combining all of the marinade ingredients together in a large bowl. To marinate the steak, squeeze the loaves gently between the palms of both hands to remove excess liquid; this will ensure that the marinade will properly soak in. You can either marinate the loaves whole (you'll need to marinate them longer, preferably a couple of days) or slice them into fillets, steaks, or chunks before marinating for 24 hours. UnSteak, in its marinade, will keep for up to 2 weeks in the refrigerator or 6 months or longer in the freezer. Defrost before using.

MAKES ABOUT 7 POUNDS

VARIATION

TRUFFLE UNSTEAK To the marinade, add 2 to 3 tablespoons of your favorite white truffle oil, plus an optional ½ cup of olive oil. Truffle seitan steak or medallions—it doesn't get much better!

PANKO BREAD CRUMBS

Panko bread crumbs are light, dry, and flaky bread crumbs originally from Japan. Actually, the words are redundant, because *panko* means "bread crumbs" in Japanese. It's like saying "bread crumb bread crumbs." But you get the point. It's great as a binder that helps absorb excess liquids and to coat everything from croquettes to Fab Cakes (page 109).

HOW TO USE UNSTEAK

Use UnSteak for any recipe that calls for beef—you can grind it in the food processor to make ground "beef," cube it, fillet it, roll it, and stuff it. Try it sautéed in a little oil on both sides with a splash of marinade to deglaze the pan for a succulent sandwich, or turn it into "veal Parmesan" or into chunks for "stroganoff." The marinade itself can be added to soups, sauces, vegetables, and grains to add flavor and umami. Keep experimenting, and you'll find a multitude of uses for it, or try the meatloaf recipe below.

a vegan tribute to my mom's meatloaf

My mom knew how to cook only Japanese food until we had lived in the United States for a few years. A neighbor kindly taught her how to make basic American dishes, and meatloaf was one that my mom mastered. This is my vegan tribute to my mom, for her meatloaf that made her so proud.

1 onion, diced

Oil or water, for sautéing

3 tablespoons whole or ground chia seeds

1½ pounds UnSteak (page 127)

1 cup panko bread crumbs (see sidebar, page 128)

3 tablespoons tomato paste

2 tablespoons soy sauce

1 teaspoons dried basil

1 teaspoon dried rosemary

1 teaspoon rubbed sage

½ teaspoon freshly ground black pepper

½ cup ketchup, preferably Maple Balsamic Ketchup (page 25) or Smoky Ketchup (page 25)

Preheat the oven to 375°F. Sauté the onion in a little oil until tender. Grind the chia seeds in a blender or coffee grinder until almost a powder (if using ground chia seeds, there is no need to grind). Cube the UnSteak, then put it in the food processor and pulse until it resembles roughly ground meat. Do not overprocess, or it will be ground too fine or into a paste and will lose the desired chewy texture. Transfer the UnSteak to a large mixing bowl and combine it with the onion, bread crumbs, tomato paste, chia seeds, soy sauce, herbs, and pepper. Prepare a loaf pan or casserole dish by oiling it or spraying lightly with a nonstick spray, and form the UnSteak mixture into a loaf with your hands. Spread the ketchup on top. Cover the pan with aluminum foil and bake for 1 hour and 15 minutes, until firm. Let it sit for at least 30 minutes before slicing and serving.

MAKES 6 TO 8 SERVINGS

italian neatballs

If you're looking for something meaty that doesn't rely on gluten or soy, give these versatile guys a whirl. You can season as you like and easily transform it into a meatloaf or burgers as well. Based on a recipe for Swedish meatballs created by blogger, author, and activist Marla Rose for her blog, *Vegan Street*, these flavorful balls derive their texture from whole grains and legumes, making them super healthy. They are baked, not fried, and come out of the oven crispy on the outside, but a brief simmering in sauce (like the Porcini Bolognese on page 145) will soften the exterior, yielding perfect tender balls with a chewy bite. Spaghetti and meatballs, anyone?

---

1 onion, diced

Oil, for sautéing (optional)

8 ounces mushrooms, quartered

2 tablespoons tamari or soy sauce

1 tablespoon chickpea miso or white miso

2 cups cooked brown rice

1 cup cooked lentils

¼ cup tomato paste

3 tablespoons nutritional yeast

4 to 6 cloves garlic, minced

1½ teaspoons dried basil

1 teaspoon fresh rosemary, chopped, or ½ teaspoon dried rosemary

½ cup rolled oats

1 cup ground walnuts (grind in a food processor), or 1½ cups gluten-free or regular bread crumbs

2 to 3 tablespoons water (if using bread crumbs)

Preheat the oven to 350°F. Line two baking sheets with parchment paper. Heat a deep skillet over medium heat and cook the onions, dry (you can sauté in oil as well, if you like), until they begin to stick a bit. Splash them with a bit of water to loosen them from the pan and continue cooking, adding a bit of water now and then to prevent sticking, until they are tender. Put the mushrooms into a food processor and pulse until they are finely minced but not reduced to a pulp. Add them to the onion and cook for several minutes, until browned. Stir in the tamari and miso.

Add the brown rice and lentils and mix well. Mix in the tomato paste, nutritional yeast, 4 cloves garlic (or more, depending on how garlicky you like it), and herbs. In a blender, process the oats briefly, but not to a flour, and add to the mixture.

continued ⟩

Now, decide whether to use walnuts or bread crumbs—walnuts will make a richer meatball, but bread crumbs will yield a more traditional texture. If using bread crumbs, sprinkle them with the water to moisten first. Mix the walnuts or moistened bread crumbs into the mixture well and form into meatballs. This can be done efficiently using a small ice cream scoop. Place on the baking sheets with ½ inch of space between them, and bake for 30 to 35 minutes, until browned and they hold their shape. Italian Neatballs will keep for 1 week in the refrigerator.

MAKES 36 BALLS

the real burger (aka now and zen burger)

What we all need is just one basic recipe for a big batch of tasty burgers that can be made ahead and stored, one that is not affected by long periods of freezing, one that you can take to nonvegan barbecues, and one that doesn't crumble if you toss it around a bit on the grill. This is another recipe that takes me back to the days of my little bistro in San Francisco, where we had many "devotees" of this simple burger, including several celebrities. There was one couple who made monthly trips from Monterey just to have these delightful patties. They are juicy, savory, chewy, and completely oil-free and go with all sorts of sauces. I get more requests from omnivores for this burger than for just about anything else. I always have a few in my freezer, just in case we need a quick meal.

---

2 pounds white or cremini mushrooms, quartered

2 large onions, diced

4 cups cooked brown rice

½ cup tomato paste

1 cup chopped parsley

⅓ cup soy sauce

3 tablespoons white or chickpea miso

1½ tablespoons dried basil

1 teaspoon dried thyme

1 teaspoon dried savory

¼ teaspoon ground allspice

3 cups vital wheat gluten

SERVING SUGGESTIONS (OPTIONAL)

⅓ cup Dijon Mustard (page 21) or a store-bought variety

3 to 4 tablespoons maple syrup or agave

1 onion, sliced

Oil, for sautéing

Burger buns

Classic Eggless Mayonnaise (page 16)
Lemon Cashew Mayo (page 18),
or Oil-Free Eggless Mayo (page 19)

Lettuce leaves or microgreens

Tomatos, sliced

Pulse the mushrooms in batches in the food processor until minced but not mushy. Transfer them to a large bowl, then mix in the onions, rice, tomato paste, parsley, soy sauce, miso, and herbs and spices. Mixing is most easily done with your hands. When everything is well incorporated, add the wheat gluten and mix well.

continued >

Preheat the oven to 350°F and grease two baking sheets or line them with parchment paper. Now form the burgers. You can just pat them into eighteen burgers with your hands, or follow one of these easy suggestions for forming:

1. Use a large ice cream scoop to form balls, drop them onto the prepared baking sheets, then flatten with your hand to form patties.

2. Find a large, deep lid for a jar, like ones often used for giant jars of peanut butter. Line it with plastic wrap. Pack in the burger mixture, then flip it out onto the prepared baking sheets (you can keep reusing the same sheet of plastic wrap). This method makes perfectly shaped burgers like the kind that come out of a box. Fool your kids with this method if they tend to clamor for "bought" goods.

Bake for about 30 minutes, until firm to the touch. Refrigerate or freeze until use. Refrigerate for a week or so or freeze for 6 to 8 months. You can reheat them in a skillet with a little oil, throw them on the grill, or pop them back in the oven.

For serving, the usual mustard and ketchup work fine, but I prefer these with some sautéed onions and a sweet Dijon sauce. To create the sauce, in a small bowl, mix together the mustard and 3 tablespoons syrup (or more, depending on how sweet you like your condiments) and set aside. In a sauté pan, sauté the sliced onion in a little oil over medium-high heat until browned. Spread burger buns with vegan mayo, place a hot burger patty on the bun, and top with a generous helping of the onions and sweet Dijon sauce. If you like, throw on some lettuce and tomatoes, too.

MAKES 18 BIG BURGERS

magic and pasta

"Life is a combination of magic and pasta."
    —Federico Fellini

I must have been Italian in my past life, because I love all things Italian. Not just my morning cappuccino or hand-rolled silky pasta, but the quirky music of the accordion, Enrico Caruso, the lilting voice of the waitress as she says *"Allora!"* and the landscape from the heel to the top of the boot. The rest of America must be as smitten, because so many Italian dishes have become staples here. What pantry doesn't have pasta of different sizes and shapes and a bottle or two of marinara? But it doesn't stop there. There's polenta and risotto (be sure to try the Roasted Tomato Risotto, page 35) and other sauces like Bolognese and vodka, most of which people don't bother to make from scratch but buy in the bottled form. While this chapter was not meant to be about Italian cuisine, I hope it will send warm Mediterranean winds into your kitchen and inspire you to try your hand at rolling some pasta or whipping up some flavorful sauces. *Buon appetito!*

15-minute rustic pasta

Probably the best place to learn how to make pasta is Italy. But if you want some homemade fettuccine tonight and aren't in Italy and don't have a pasta machine, here's the recipe for you. Start to finish, it's a 30-minute dish, including about 15 minutes of rest time. (Pictured on page 147.)

---

2 cups semolina flour, plus more for sprinkling

1 cup all-purpose flour

About 1 cup hot water

Put both flours in a food processor. Put the lid on the food processor, turn it on, and slowly pour the hot water through the spout. The mixture will first look like cornmeal, then form tiny little balls whirling around the work bowl and, finally, after a couple of minutes, form a big ball in the middle. Let it go for another 30 seconds to knead the dough, then turn it off. Remove the dough. It will be quite warm and pliable. Flatten it out into a ½-inch-thick pancake, then cut it into quarters. Cover the dough with a dry towel and let it rest for 10 to 15 minutes.

Sprinkle some semolina or all-purpose flour onto a clean, dry surface and put one of the four pieces of dough on it. Using a rolling pin, roll it out as thinly as you can (it will expand as it cooks). You can make it as thin as an envelope with a card in it, or as thick as ⅛ inch, which will create a chewy, rustic, country-style pasta.

After you've rolled out all of the sheets, use a sharp knife or pizza cutter to cut them as desired, one sheet at a time. You can cut them into any width that will suit the sauce of the evening, whether spaghetti, fettuccine, pappardelle, or lasagna.

Get that large pot of salted water boiling (about 8 cups), then cook the noodles for 2 to 3 minutes, until perfectly al dente. Serve with a sauce of your choice. To store the pasta, toss it with a little semolina or flour to prevent sticking, then wrap in plastic wrap or put in a covered container and refrigerate for 2 to 3 days.

MAKES 1½ POUNDS, ENOUGH FOR 6 TO 8 SERVINGS

VARIATION

WHOLE WHEAT PASTA Substitute 1 cup whole wheat bread flour (not whole wheat pastry flour) for the all-purpose flour.

gluten-free brown rice pasta

The glutinous rice flour in this pasta increases the chewiness of this gluten-free pasta (glutinous rice flour is gluten-free!). However, it cannot be cooked while fresh, or it will turn to mush. After letting it dry completely, however, it cooks up into a beautiful, al dente pasta!

2 cups brown rice flour

1 cup glutinous rice flour (mochiko, see sidebar), plus more for dusting

2 teaspoons xanthan gum

1 cup hot water, or more as needed

Combine the flours and xanthan gum in the food processor and add the hot water. Let the processor run for a few minutes until a ball forms in the middle. If it seems too dry or the dough doesn't come together, add 1 tablespoon of hot water at a time until it does. Process for another minute, then turn it out onto a clean surface dusted well with rice flour. Divide the dough into quarters and form four balls. Put three of them in a plastic bag to prevent drying (this dough dries out very fast!).

Pat the remaining ball into a circle about ½ inch thick. Using a rolling pin, roll it out as thin as you can get it, preferably about ⅛ inch thick. You can also use a pasta machine to roll it out and cut it. If rolling by hand, use a pizza cutter or knife to cut it into fettuccine or whatever width you want. Form a pile of noodles on top of a cooling rack or a lightly floured baking sheet; this is not a sticky dough, so you needn't worry about the noodles sticking together. Repeat with the remaining dough, one ball at a time. Let the pasta dry at room temperature for about 2 days before using. Once it is completely dry, put it in a ziplock bag and store at room temperature for 3 to 4 months. Cook for 5 to 8 minutes in boiling water, depending on thickness.

MAKES ABOUT 1½ POUNDS, ENOUGH FOR 6 TO 8 SERVINGS

GLUTINOUS RICE FLOUR

Glutinous rice flour, or mochiko in Japanese, is also known as sweet rice flour and does not contain any gluten. It's made from a variety of rice that produces a very sticky, almost gluey texture. This is the type of rice used to make mochi, the sticky Japanese rice cakes.

buckwheat pasta

The earthiness of buckwheat lends a rustic touch to this hand-rolled pasta, where the slight variance in thickness and width are part of the charm. With just a rolling pin, you'll be diving into chewy, earthy goodness in no time. As for sauces, anything creamy, like Alfredo or Vodka Sauce (page 148), will dress it nicely, but the piquant Spinach and Caper Sauce (page 149) adds an especially vibrant touch.

8 ounces regular, medium, or medium-firm tofu

1¼ cups semolina or bread flour, plus more for sprinkling

¾ cup buckwheat flour

About 1 tablespoon sea salt

Place the tofu in a food processor and process until it is creamy, although it does not have to be completely smooth; a few grainy bits are fine. Add 1 cup of the semolina and all of the buckwheat flour. Process again briefly. Add the remaining ¼ cup semolina until the dough is no longer sticky but still soft.

Remove the dough from the food processor. Sprinkle some semolina or buckwheat flour on a board or counter and knead the dough for about 10 minutes, until smooth and pliable. Cover the dough with a dry towel and let it rest for 20 to 30 minutes.

Divide the dough in half. Roll out each half until it is about ½ inch thick. Divide it in half again. Now roll each piece into a 10 by 6-inch rectangle. It should be about ⅛ inch thick. Sprinkle the top lightly with semolina and brush off any excess. Using a knife, cut each sheet of pasta into any width you like—I like it as ⅓- to ½-inch-wide pappardelle. Repeat with the other three pieces of dough. You can cook the pasta right away or set it aside for several hours. To set aside, cover it with a damp but not wet towel to prevent it from drying out. To store the pasta, toss it with a little semolina, bread flour, or buckwheat flour to prevent sticking, then wrap in plastic wrap or put in a covered container and refrigerate for 2 to 3 days.

Bring about 8 cups water to a boil and throw in the salt. Add the pasta, give it a stir to separate it and prevent sticking, and cook for 2 to 3 minutes, until tender but still chewy. Drain in a colander and serve right away with your favorite sauce.

MAKES ABOUT 1 POUND, ENOUGH FOR 4 TO 6 SERVINGS

the methodology of marinara

I live for hot summers, for tomato vines heavy with fruit bursting with flavor so sweet that I wonder if someone has secretly gone amid them at night injecting them with sugar. I honor the tomato so much that I will generally not make tomato-based dishes in the winter. How do you make a good pot of tomato sauce? Not by opening up cans of tomatoes. I don't care if they are San Marzano. There's no marinara as good as the kind that is made from the freshest, ripest tomatoes. Any other is a disservice to it. How hard is it to make your own marinara? It is the easiest thing if you have good tomatoes. Otherwise, it is nearly impossible.

So you say I have a few opinions about tomatoes. I do. A good tomato sauce is all about the tomatoes. With just a touch of salt, garlic, olive oil, and an herb or two, you should have a magnificent sauce that will make it difficult for you to stop eating that plate of pasta in front of you. It's only when the tomatoes are less than stellar—or canned—that you need to simmer them for hours and mask them with all sorts of other things. But then I don't think it's worth eating.

Throughout the countryside of Italy, I did not tire of plates of pasta pomodoro, no matter how many times I had it. Just some simple pasta with a fresh tomato sauce, and I was in heaven every time. This is how it should be. How can you make this happen year-round? I recommend that when the tomato harvest is in, you get a bunch. Grow them yourself or go to the farmers' market (be sure to taste the tomatoes before buying pounds and pounds!). At the end of summer, sometimes they practically give them away. You can get the ones that are soft, almost oozing with juice (just make sure they haven't gone bad). You can even use cherry tomatoes, which produce really sweet sauce. Any shape, size, or color of tomato works, but they must be ripe. Turn them into sauce and store it in the freezer. It's like freezing the flavor of summer to enjoy all throughout the other seasons.

---

4 pounds fresh, ripe tomatoes, any variety

3 tablespoons extra-virgin olive oil

5 or 6 cloves garlic, minced

1 teaspoon sea salt

Several sprigs fresh basil or rosemary

The sweeter the tomatoes, the sweeter your sauce, so be sure to taste them first! You don't need to remove the skins, and you can employ one of several ways to cut them up. If they are really ripe, I sometimes just take them in my hands and squeeze them, a trick I learned from an Italian cooking show when I was a teenager. I throw it all in—skins, seeds, juice, flesh. Or you can chop them up roughly or pulse them in the food processor so that they're chunky. If they are cherry tomatoes, just cut them in half or pulse briefly in a food processor after removing the stems (or do nothing at all—just leave them whole!).

Now get a large, heavy pan—I prefer a wide, deep skillet, chef's pan, or Dutch oven so that the sauce has more surface area and cooks quickly, as opposed to a deep pot with a smaller surface area. Heat the pan over medium heat, add the olive oil, and then once heated throw in the minced garlic—the amount provided here is just a guideline; you can feel free to add more or less. Let the garlic sizzle for a minute, then add the tomatoes and salt and let it simmer for 20 to 30 minutes, stirring frequently, until it has reduced some and developed a saucelike consistency. Adjust the seasonings as desired. The deeper and narrower the pot, the longer it will take—maybe even 40 minutes, but in a deep skillet, it should take no more than 20. You can leave it slightly chunky or use an immersion blender to puree it as you like.

Finally, to add that final bit of fragrance, throw in a small handful of slivered fresh basil leaves or a sprig or two of fresh rosemary. Basil is sweet and traditional, but rosemary can add a wonderful savory quality that's beautiful over richer dishes, like a parmigiana. Let the sauce simmer for another minute. Taste it. You should be singing. Marinara will keep for about a week in the refrigerator. To store it longer so that you can enjoy it until the next tomato season, put it in a plastic container and freeze, where it should keep all year long until the next harvest.

MAKES ABOUT 5 CUPS, ENOUGH FOR 4 TO 6 SERVINGS

CUSTOMIZE YOUR MARINARA

You can easily adapt this recipe to any quantity you want. It's really a general method, so feel free to double it, halve it, use more or less garlic, or even no oil. It's up to you— and the tomatoes.

porcini bolognese sauce

Here is my answer for a rich, hearty, and—dare I say—"meaty" sauce for pasta. I've found that the trick is infusing the seitan with flavor before adding the tomatoes and other ingredients. Pureed porcini mushrooms add a deep, woodsy flavor, catapulting this classic sauce to new heights that will satisfy even the fussiest carnivore.

1½ pounds UnSteak (page 127)

1 cup hot water

¾ cup dried porcini mushrooms

¼ cup olive oil or water, or more as needed

1 onion, diced

8 cloves garlic (at least!), minced

3 tablespoons soy sauce or tamari

2 tablespoons white, chickpea, or yellow miso

1 (28-ounce) can plum tomatoes, pulsed in a blender or food processor, or equivalent of fresh, very ripe tomatoes

½ cup red wine, or more as needed

¼ cup tomato paste

2 teaspoons dried basil, or about ¼ cup loosely packed fresh basil leaves

1 teaspoons dried rosemary, or 1 or 2 sprigs fresh rosemary

Cut the UnSteak into 1-inch chunks and process briefly in a food processor to resemble ground beef. Do not overprocess, or it could end up too fine or pureed and lose all of its texture. Pour the hot water over the porcini mushrooms in a small bowl and set aside for 15 minutes, until fully reconstituted. Puree the mushrooms and their liquid in the food processor to form a thick slurry.

Heat the oil in a large, deep sauté pan over medium heat and sauté the onion and garlic until tender. Add the ground UnSteak, soy sauce, miso, and pureed porcinis. Mix well, and simmer for about 15 minutes, until the UnSteak has absorbed most of the liquid. Add the chopped tomatoes, red wine, and tomato paste. If you are using dried herbs, add them now, too. Partly cover and simmer for about 30 minutes, until the sauce looks divinely delicious. If you're using fresh herbs, add them to the sauce during the last 10 minutes of cooking. Porcini Bolognese is best if allowed to sit for several hours to allow the flavors to meld and develop. Make it a day ahead of time if desired. Stored in a covered container, it will keep for about 1 week in the refrigerator or several months in the freezer.

MAKES 8 SERVINGS

umbrian tartufo sauce

Several years ago, I spent a couple of luxurious weeks in the Umbrian town of Assisi. The first thing I noticed was a regional specialty on every menu—*strangozzi al tartufo*. When I took my first bite of the rough-hewn, hand-pulled pasta tossed with aromatic, minced truffles cooked with copious amounts of olive oil and garlic, I wanted to run to the Basilica and kiss the feet of Saint Francis. I became obsessed with this dish and tried it everywhere. Here is the poor man's version, sans real truffles, but still tasty enough to make me recall that wondrous time in the hills of Umbria. And with the drastically reduced amount of olive oil (which I've replaced with cashew cream), I can enjoy it more often as well. Of course, feel free to pour on the oil for a more authentic version.

---

1 pound cremini mushrooms

1 to 2 tablespoons extra-virgin olive oil (optional)

½ cup minced shallot

6 cloves garlic, minced

2 to 3 tablespoons good-quality white truffle oil, or to taste

1 cup Cashew Cream (page 56)

Sea salt and freshly ground black pepper

10 ounces cooked spaghetti or strangozzi, if you can get it, or homemade pasta (page 138)

Parsley, for garnish (optional)

Cut the mushrooms in half or quarters, depending on how large they are, so they are all fairly uniform in size. Pulse them in a food processor until they are finely minced but not mushy. Be sure not to process too long, or you will end up with a puree.

In a large skillet over medium-high heat, heat the oil. Add the shallot and sauté until tender. For oil-free cooking, simply sauté the shallot with a dash of water. Add the garlic and mushrooms and sauté for 5 to 10 minutes, until the mushrooms are browned and moist but not wet looking. Add the truffle oil and cashew cream and stir well. Cook for 1 minute to let the sauce thicken, then season with salt and pepper. Toss with hot spaghetti, garnish with some chopped parsley, and serve immediately. Best enjoyed when freshly made; leftovers can be stored in a covered container in the refrigerator for 2 or 3 days. Do not freeze, or it will change the texture.

MAKES 4 SERVINGS

Umbrian Tartufo Sauce with 15-Minute
Rustic Pasta (page 138)

vodka sauce

This creamy sauce has just enough sophistication to please both adults and kids alike. Although traditionally served over penne pasta, it's great on a pizza as well as over baked potatoes.

---

2 tablespoons Glorious Butterless Butter (page 58)

1 large onion, minced

3 cloves garlic

½ cup vodka

1 (28-ounce) can pureed or diced tomatoes

¼ cup tomato paste

2 cups Cashew Cream (page 56)

2 tablespoons nutritional yeast

Sea salt and freshly ground black pepper

In a deep skillet over medium heat, melt the butter and sauté the onion until tender. Add the garlic and sauté for another minute. Then add the vodka and simmer for about 5 minutes. Next, add the tomatoes and tomato paste and simmer for about 10 minutes, stirring occasionally. Finally, add the cashew cream and nutritional yeast, season with salt and pepper, and simmer on low for a few minutes to let the flavors meld. Serve immediately with pasta or a side of your choice or store it in a covered container in the refrigerator for 1 week or, like marinara, for many, many months in the freezer.

MAKES 4 TO 6 SERVINGS

VARIATION
OIL-FREE VODKA SAUCE Omit the butter and simply sauté the onion in a bit of water.

spinach and caper sauce

This vibrant, piquant green sauce looks like pesto but delivers up a lovely bite from the capers. It's also oil-free and far more nutrient-dense than its sister pesto. A whole head of spinach goes into this sauce, so it's a great way to eat your veggies. And it's raw, with no need to heat, so it takes but 30 seconds to whip up! Serve over any kind of pasta, although it is particularly good over Buckwheat Pasta (page 140).

½ cup cashews

1½ cups water

½ cup raw walnuts

4 or 5 cloves garlic

¼ cup capers

1 cup loosely packed cilantro

1 cup loosely packed fresh basil leaves

1 bunch spinach, washed well and roughly chopped

Sea salt

Place the cashews and water in a blender and process until very creamy and smooth. Remove about ½ cup of this cashew cream and set aside. You may or may not need all of it. Add the walnuts, 4 cloves of garlic (or more, depending on how garlicky you like it), capers, cilantro, and basil to the blender and pulse briefly to chop. Add the spinach a handful at a time until it is incorporated. If the sauce is very thick, you can add the remaining cashew cream, or you can make it lower in fat by adding water from cooking your pasta. It should have a thick but pourable consistency. Season to taste with salt, and adjust the other seasonings as well, adding another tablespoon of capers, a clove of garlic, or more basil as desired. Toss with hot pasta and serve. Spinach and Caper Sauce is best eaten when freshly made. You can keep leftovers in a covered container in the refrigerator for a day or two.

MAKES ABOUT 4 CUPS, ENOUGH FOR 4 TO 6 SERVINGS

well-crafted macaroni and cheese mix

Unless you were raised by macrobiotic hippies, you've had it. I've had it. And there's no shame in saying it—we've all had macaroni and cheese out of the box. My kids would plead with me to buy it, and I was thrilled when the vegan stuff came on the market. Maybe you don't crave it anymore, but it sure is convenient to have some on hand for the kids or the babysitter. But there's no need to buy it, because you can make the instant cheese sauce mix yourself in just a few minutes! This version is richer than the variation that follows, utilizing glorious cashews.

1 cup cashews

¾ cup nutritional yeast

¼ cup oat flour (see sidebar, page 162)

¼ cup tapioca flour

1 tablespoon paprika

1 tablespoon organic sugar

2 teaspoons powdered mustard

2 teaspoons sea salt

2 teaspoons onion powder

Add all of the ingredients to a food processor and process until a powder is formed. There should not be any discernible chunks or large granules of cashews, so this may take 3 to 4 minutes of processing. Store this in a jar or portion out into ⅓-cup increments and put in ziplock bags and store in the pantry for a month or two or in the refrigerator for up to 6 months.

MAKES 1⅔ CUPS, OR ENOUGH TO COAT THE EQUIVALENT OF 5 STORE-BOUGHT BOXES INSTANT MACARONI AND CHEESE

VARIATION

NUT-FREE WELL-CRAFTED MACARONI AND CHEESE MIX This is similar to the recipe above, but it's nut-free and therefore lower in fat. Omit the cashews and increase the oat flour to ¾ cup. Reduce the sugar to 1½ teaspoons and the powdered mustard to 1 teaspoon. Add all of the ingredients to a food processor and process until thoroughly mixed. Store this in a jar or portion out into ⅓-cup increments and put in ziplock bags and keep it in the pantry for 2 to 3 months.

continued ⤳

HOW TO USE WELL-CRAFTED MACARONI AND CHEESE MIX

Cook 1 cup of dry macaroni according to package instructions and drain. Combine ⅓ cup mix with 1 cup water or unsweetened nondairy milk in a saucepan over medium-low heat. Whisk well and bring to a boil. Simmer for 1 minute, then toss with the hot cooked macaroni.

These mixes are also a great answer for turning yesterday's leftovers into a quick casserole. Just combine leftover pasta, potatoes, or grains, some veggies, and any other odd scraps you think might be a good fit and mix it in a casserole dish with some of the cheese mix and water. You can add more spices and herbs if you wish. Then bake it all up into creamy goodness. You can also use the mix to make quick sauces for veggies or add it to soups for extra cheesy flavor and richness—it's quite versatile.

silky mac 'n' cheese sauce

If you have the Oil-Free Melty "Cheddar" (page 73) on hand, this cheese sauce comes together in a jiffy and is made in the traditional manner of melting cheese in hot milk. It creates a smooth, creamy, silky texture that can be tossed with macaroni or penne or poured over a baked potato.

---

2 cups unsweetened nondairy milk

8 ounces Oil-Free Melty "Cheddar" (page 73)

Pour the milk into a medium saucepan over medium heat. Meanwhile, cut the Cheddar into ½-inch cubes and toss into the milk. Whisk the mixture until the cheese has melted completely and the sauce is thickened. Serve over cooked pasta of your choice. This makes enough for about 4 cups of cooked pasta. Stored in a covered container, this sauce will keep for about 1 week in the refrigerator, or it can be frozen for several months.

MAKES 2 CUPS, ENOUGH FOR 3 OR 4 SERVINGS OR 4 CUPS COOKED PASTA

oven-cooked polenta

So you say you don't like those flavorless tubes of polenta from the store? But think homemade is just too much trouble? Well, I'm here to tell you that you've been liberated from the stove—just let your oven do all the work! I first learned of this method from a local food writer, who got it from a cookbook, whose author found it on the back of a polenta box. So there you have it. A bit of nutritional yeast and garlic will flavor it so that it becomes a tasty base for all sorts of toppings, or it can be used in lasagna instead of pasta.

10 cups water

2 cups dry polenta (coarse cornmeal)

2 teaspoons sea salt

¼ cup nutritional yeast

6 to 12 cloves garlic, minced

Preheat the oven to 350°F. Put the water in a large ovenproof pot or Dutch oven and bring it to a boil over high heat. Whisk in the polenta and salt. Cover the pot and put it in the oven. Bake for about 30 minutes, until it has thickened some, then remove and stir in the nutritional yeast and 6 cloves garlic (or more, depending on how garlicky you like it). Continue baking for another 20 minutes or so, until the mixture is thick, smooth, and creamy.

You can enjoy it right away as soft polenta or pour it into an oiled dish—a rimmed baking sheet, baking dish, casserole, or whatever shape you want—and let it harden at room temperature or in the refrigerator. It can take anywhere from 30 minutes to a couple of hours to firm up, depending on how thick the layer is and whether it's cooled at room temperature or in the refrigerator. When firm, you can slice it or cut it with cookie cutters into cute shapes and then panfry or bake until crispy on the outside and creamy in the middle. Polenta is best stored in a covered container in the fridge and eaten within 1 week. To reheat, slice it as desired and sauté both sides until browned. It's best not to freeze polenta, as the texture changes.

MAKES 6 TO 8 SERVINGS AS AN ENTRÉE, OR 12 TO 20 APPETIZERS

CUSTOMIZE YOUR POLENTA

There are lots of goodies that can be thrown in to enhance flavor and add textures—you can use your imagination (and the contents of your fridge) to customize your polenta, but here are some tips: Fresh herbs, such as rosemary and basil, are wonderful, as are sun-dried tomatoes or Roasted Tomatoes (page 33). All of the sausage recipes in this book (and what a good use for a stray leftover sausage or two!) are great in this, especially combined with some sautéed fresh chard or other greens. Add the enhancements to the polenta during the last 10 to 15 minutes in the oven or at the same time you add the nutritional yeast and garlic. And finally, a little homemade cheese can be stirred in at the last minute to add flavor and richness.

the grains of truth

It seems like half of this country has a fear of carbohydrates, thinking it will make them fat. When they order sandwiches, they ask for it sans bread (Can I have it between lettuce, please?). Bread baskets at restaurants go untouched. But when I was in Kyoto giving a talk, I asked the members of my Japanese audience if they thought rice would make them fat. They looked utterly puzzled. What the heck was I talking about? When I told them of the American trend of shunning carbs, they chuckled politely. Among this packed room of rice eaters, there was not an overweight person to be seen. In just about every country but ours, grains are the staple food, the thing that takes up the most space on their plates. And what are their rates of obesity? Practically nonexistent.

I just hope that as a country we get past this crazy fear of starches soon. Whether rice, pasta, corn, or lesser known grains like farro, starches provide not only energy to get through our day but also protein, fiber, and phytonutrients. They also provide satiety, and you can't knock that. Best of all, they are comforting, feeding our souls as well as our bodies.

Of course, it's always preferable to eat whole grains, so I encourage you to fill your plates with brown rice, quinoa, and whole corn. But let's face it—there's a time and place for a crusty baguette, too. Unfortunately, grain-based products are often the most processed ones on the market, making them less than a desirable option. So dip your hand into the flour bin and make them yourself. You'll find that things like pancake mix, energy bars, and granola are not only easy to whip up, but also tastier than what you can buy at the store. Why not impress your friends with homemade crackers at holiday time? Or if you're tired of spending several bucks a loaf for some bread, spend just several minutes in your kitchen to make your own. And good old pizza? If you're tired of paying a premium to the delivery man for a cheeseless pizza, learn the trick to making your own chewy, thin-crust wonder that you can top with anything. How about some vegan "mozzarella" (page 72)?

classic pancake and biscuit mix

Weekends are more relaxing with this in your cupboard ready to be
turned into pancakes, biscuits, and waffles.

4 cups all-purpose flour

5 tablespoons ground flax seeds

3 tablespoons organic sugar

2 tablespoons baking powder

½ teaspoon sea salt

Combine all of the ingredients in a large bowl and whisk until thoroughly combined,
2 to 3 minutes. Store in an airtight container or ziplock bags in your pantry for up
to 6 months.

MAKES 4½ CUPS

VARIATION

WHOLE WHEAT PANCAKE AND BISCUIT MIX Substitute whole wheat pastry flour
for the all-purpose flour and increase the baking powder to 3 tablespoons. Follow the
ratios below for pancakes and waffles.

Whole Wheat Pancakes—1½ parts baking mix : 1 part soy milk

Whole Wheat Waffles—1 part baking mix : 1 part soy milk

If desired, add 1 tablespoon of maple syrup at the same time as the soy milk for
extra sweetness.

HOW TO USE CLASSIC PANCAKE AND BISCUIT MIX

diner pancakes

These are thick, fluffy pancakes that will delight young and old alike, bringing back memories of a slower time when Sunday mornings were lazy and meant for lounging in pajamas. And these pancakes let you stay in your pajamas, because they're so easy to make once you have the mix! The recipe is just equal parts mix and nondairy milk, so you can make this in any quantity you want. As a guide, 1 cup of mix is enough for 4 to 6 pancakes, so that might feed two or three people (or sometimes only one!).

1 cup Classic Pancake and Biscuit Mix (page 158)

1 cup nondairy milk

1 teaspoon vanilla extract (optional)

Glorious Butterless Butter (page 58), for serving

Maple syrup, for serving

Heat the griddle over medium heat before you mix the batter. Your griddle should be nice and hot when the batter hits it. To make the batter, simply put the mix, nondairy milk, and vanilla in a medium to large bowl and stir quickly but not thoroughly; you want to leave it a little lumpy. Right before you cook, spray the griddle with a little nonstick spray or melt a little Glorious Butterless Butter on it. Then pour ⅓ to ½ cup of batter per pancake. To make light, fluffy pancakes, be sure to cook them on one side until the top is covered in bubbles (air pockets), then flip and cook briefly until browned. If they seem to be browning too quickly, turn down the heat. They'll rise quite a bit, so three of them will form a generous stack. Spread on some Glorious Butterless Butter, pour on some maple syrup, and dig in while in your jammies!

MAKES 4 TO 6 PANCAKES

continued ⟩

fluffy biscuits

These biscuits are as light as air with a delicate crumb. (Pictured opposite, and on page 59.)

2 cups Classic Pancake and Biscuit Mix (page 158)

⅓ cup cold Glorious Butterless Butter (page 58), cut into ½-inch pieces

¾ cup nondairy milk

1 teaspoon apple cider vinegar

Preheat the oven to 400°F. Line a baking sheet with parchment paper. Put the mix and butter in a medium bowl, and using a pastry cutter or a fork, work the butter into the flour so that it resembles cornmeal. Form a well in the center, pour in the milk and vinegar, and lightly stir to combine. It doesn't need to be smooth; the dough should be rough looking. Use a spoon to drop lumps of the dough onto the baking sheet and bake for about 15 minutes, until lightly golden. Biscuits are best hot out of the oven! If you want to keep them around for a day or two, let them cool completely, then store in a ziplock bag at room temperature. Then reheat in the oven to refresh them.

MAKES 12 BISCUITS

crispy waffles

These light, classic waffles are a sweet start to a weekend morning.

1 cup Classic Pancake and Biscuit Mix (page 158)

1¼ cups nondairy milk

1 tablespoon maple syrup (optional)

Preheat a waffle iron. Lightly whisk together the mix and nondairy milk in a medium bowl. Add the maple syrup to the mixture for extra sweetness. Pour into the heated waffle iron and cook until crispy and golden brown on both sides.

MAKES 2 TO 4 WAFFLES, DEPENDING ON WAFFLE IRON

buckwheat pancake and waffle mix

This has become my go-to mix for weekends when we want something more than a smoothie. It produces the lightest and crispiest waffles, and pancakes with an earthy, yet not overwhelming, buckwheat flavor. Having this on hand in my pantry makes it easy to whip up a healthy but special breakfast whenever I want.

2 cups buckwheat flour

4 cups oat flour (see sidebar)

⅓ cup coconut sugar, or ¼ cup organic sugar

6 tablespoons ground flax seeds

5 tablespoons baking powder

1 tablespoon ground cinnamon

1½ teaspoons sea salt

Combine all of the ingredients in a large bowl and, using a wire whisk, stir continuously for a couple of minutes to mix thoroughly. If desired, the mixing can be done in a food processor or an electric mixer instead. Store in an airtight container at room temperature for 3 to 4 months.

MAKES ABOUT 2 POUNDS, OR ABOUT 7 CUPS

OAT FLOUR

If oat flour is unavailable at your local grocery store, you can make it easily at home. Simply grind rolled oats in a blender until reduced to a fine flour.

HOW TO USE BUCKWHEAT PANCAKE AND WAFFLE MIX

waffles

Where you would expect earthy and heavy, these waffles are ever so light and crispy.

1 cup nondairy milk

1 teaspoon vanilla extract

1 cup Buckwheat Pancake and Waffle Mix (page 162)

Combine the milk and vanilla in a medium bowl, then whisk in the mix with a few strokes until combined. The mixture will seem thin. Let it sit for a few minutes while the waffle iron heats up; it will thicken a bit. Heat the waffle iron according to the manufacturer's instructions and brush lightly with oil or spray with a nonstick spray. Pour the mixture into the iron and cook until crispy and brown.

crepes

Thin, delicate, flavorful crepes work beautifully to encase everything from creamed mushrooms to apple compote.

1 cup Buckwheat Pancake and Waffle Mix (page 162)

½ teaspoon xanthan gum

2 cups water

In a large bowl, whisk together the mix, xanthan gum, and water. The batter should be thin, but thick enough to coat the back of a spoon. Heat an 8- to 10-inch crepe pan or a nonstick skillet over low heat. Spray it with nonstick spray or let a knob of Glorious Butterless Butter (page 58) melt all around it. Pour ¼ to ⅓ cup of batter onto the pan and quickly swirl the pan around, tilting it around so that the mixture spreads and coats the entire pan in a thin layer. Cook until bubbles form all over the top and the bottom is brown. Carefully flip it over and cook for about 20 seconds on the other side. Repeat, stacking the crepes on a plate, until the batter is gone.

MAKES 10 TO 12 CREPES

continued ⟶

beer pancakes

These take me back to my first restaurant gig in high school, when I'd get up at 5:00 a.m. to get to work on time for breakfast service. Beer pancakes were the blue plate special at this place in Sausalito, and I had my share of them.

1 cup plus 2 tablespoons Buckwheat Pancake and Waffle Mix (page 162)

1¼ cups beer (not stout or dark beer, but just about anything else works)

1 teaspoon apple cider vinegar

Glorious Butterless Butter (page 58), for serving

Maple syrup, for serving

Put the mix in a medium bowl, make a well in the center, and pour the beer and vinegar into it. Whisk it a few times to mix. The mixture may seem thin; it will thicken as it sits for a few minutes. Heat a griddle over medium heat until hot, then grease lightly with Glorious Butterless Butter or spray with a nonstick spray. Spoon about ¼ cup per pancake onto the hot griddle and flip the pancake over after the surface is covered with bubbles (not before!). Cook on both sides until brown. Serve with Glorious Butterless Butter and maple syrup.

MAKES 4 TO 6 PANCAKES

oil-free superfood granola

While the next recipe is your standard granola recipe, this is the one I typically make and eat. It's what my friend Chef AJ would call unprocessed—there's no oil, sugar, or salt in this recipe. I love it atop a bowl of fresh fruit and yogurt, and it'll keep me energized all morning. Of course, you can vary the "additions" to your liking or just follow this precisely. AJ, I dedicate this recipe to you!

---

3 cups rolled oats

½ cup almond meal

½ cup pumpkin seeds

½ cup chopped walnuts, pecans, or almonds

½ cup shredded coconut

3 tablespoons flax seeds

3 tablespoons chia seeds

3 tablespoons sesame seeds

1 tablespoon vanilla extract

1 teaspoon ground cinnamon

½ teaspoon ground cardamom

1½ cup dates, soaked in water to cover overnight, ¼ cup soaking liquid reserved

¾ cup dried blueberries, cranberries, currants, or raisins

½ cup goji berries (optional)

Preheat the oven to 250°F and line a baking sheet with parchment paper. In a large bowl, combine the oats, almond meal, pumpkin seeds, nuts, coconut, flax seeds, chia seeds, sesame seeds, vanilla, cinnamon, and cardamom. In a blender, puree the soaked dates with the reserved soaking liquid. Mix into the oat mixture to coat the oats thoroughly.

Spread onto the baking sheet and bake for about 1½ hours, until golden brown, stirring the mixture every 20 minutes or so to ensure even baking. Let cool completely, then mix in the dried fruit. Store in an airtight container at room temperature for 6 to 8 weeks.

Note: This can also be made in a dehydrator at 115°F. It will take 24 hours or more. If desired, any of the seeds or nuts can be omitted.

MAKES 6 TO 7 CUPS

granola unleashed

Read the ingredients on a bag of granola sometime, and you'll realize that there's no reason not to make your own at home. All you need is this simple methodology. Here, you'll find the recipe for a basic granola and then a list of all of the ways you can change it up and make it your very own. Who knows ... maybe you'll find your own custom blend and end up selling it at your local farmers' market.

⅓ cup canola or other neutral vegetable oil

½ cup maple syrup

½ teaspoon sea salt

3 cups rolled oats

Preheat the oven to 325°F. Line a baking sheet with parchment paper. In a large mixing bowl, combine the oil, maple syrup, and salt and mix well. Add the oats and stir well to coat the oats thoroughly. Spread on the pan and bake for 20 minutes. Remove from the oven and, using a spatula, stir the mixture to ensure even baking. Put it back in the oven and bake for another 20 minutes, stir again, and bake for a final 15 to 20 minutes, until golden brown. It will become crisp as it cools. Store in an airtight container for 6 to 8 weeks.

MAKES 3½ CUPS

VARIATIONS

THE LESS SWEET VERSION Increase oats by 1 cup.

NUTTY SEEDY BLENDS To the oats in either the basic granola recipe or Less Sweet Version, mix in any or all of the following: ¼ cup flax seeds; ¼ cup chia seeds; ¾ cup chopped almonds, walnuts, pecans, hazelnuts; ½ cup sesame seeds; ½ cup pumpkin seeds.

VANILLA ALMOND BLUEBERRY To the oil–maple syrup mixture in the basic granola recipe or Less Sweet Version, add 1 tablespoon vanilla and ½ teaspoon almond extract. Then along with the oats add ½ cup sliced almonds. Finally, after baking, mix in ¾ cup dried blueberries.

MAPLE NUT CINNAMON RAISIN To the oats in the basic granola recipe, add 2 teaspoons ground cinnamon and ¾ cup chopped walnuts. After baking, mix in 1 cup raisins.

mountain bars

There was a time in my life when I should have bought stock in a particular energy bar company. Between all the members of my family, we spent a small fortune on them, frequently eating them in place of meals. It didn't occur to us that they were high in sugar and calories, and that while perhaps they were fine as an occasional snack when hiking, they weren't really a substitute for a real food—like a sweet potato!

But there is a time and place for them. Like when you're on that long hike. Or a long bike ride, and you just want to be able to reach into your backpack and fuel yourself for the rest of the ride home. Here's a recipe that's easy to whip up and flexible with the flavors, so you can have that variety pack. They're chewy and good, while not being overly sweet, so you won't mistake them for cookies and eat the whole batch. And because they're supposed to provide you with energy and nutrition, I've kept them minimally processed, using only whole ingredients for a sustained release of energy. After all, when that big hill looms in front of you and you're wiping the sweat from your brow, that's what you want, right?

2 tablespoons ground flax seeds

⅓ cup water

1 cup pitted dates

1 cup mashed ripe bananas (about 2)

⅓ cup brown rice syrup

⅓ cup shredded coconut

¼ cup hemp seeds

¼ cup pumpkin seeds (optional)

2 tablespoons chia seeds

1 teaspoon vanilla extract

1½ cups rolled oats

Preheat the oven to 350°F. Line a baking sheet with parchment paper. Mix the flax seeds with the water in a small bowl and set aside for a few minutes to thicken. In a food processor, combine the dates, bananas, and brown rice syrup and puree until smooth. Add the flax mixture and process again. Transfer this to a large mixing bowl and stir in the remaining ingredients. Drop the mixture onto the baking sheet in 2- to 3-tablespoon-size portions and form into bar shapes. Bake for 15 to 25 minutes, depending on the flavor (see Variations). Let them cool before eating.

They will keep at room temperature for 3 to 4 days in an airtight container, but for longer storage, store in the freezer in ziplock bags where they will keep for several months. If you put them in individual ziplock bags, you can grab them when you leave the house and they will be thawed and ready to eat by the time you need one on that hike!

MAKES 12 TO 18 BARS

VARIATIONS

CHOCOLATE CHIP Add ½ cup chocolate chips to the mixture. Bake for 15 to 20 minutes, until golden brown.

DOUBLE CHOCOLATE CHIP Add ½ cup chocolate chips and ¼ cup cocoa powder. Bake for about 15 minutes, until browned and dry to the touch.

CARROT CAKE Add 2 grated carrots, ½ cup raisins, ¼ cup chopped walnuts, 1 teaspoon ground cinnamon, 1 teaspoon ground ginger, and ¼ teaspoon ground cardamom. Bake for 20 to 25 minutes, until golden brown and dry to the touch.

PEANUT BUTTER Add ¾ cup peanut butter to the date mixture in the food processor. If you like, go ahead and throw in ½ cup chocolate chips, too! Bake for about 15 minutes, until golden brown.

APPLE PIE Replace the bananas with 1 cup applesauce. Add 1 teaspoon ground cinnamon and ¼ teaspoon ground nutmeg. Bake for about 25 minutes, until golden brown and dry to the touch.

PROTEIN POWER Add 2 scoops plain or vanilla vegan protein powder (your pick! I like pea protein) to any of the flavor variations. Baking time will be about 5 minutes less than indicated for each particular flavor; bake until golden brown.

gluten-free crunchy polenta and seed crackers

I serve cheese platters to people all the time, which means I always have to have gluten-free cracker options on hand. This recipe and my Delicate Flax Seed Crackers (page 171, with truffle oil and herbes de Provence) are my go-to choice for gluten-free options that don't taste like rice crackers.

1 cup brown rice flour

¼ cup oat flour (see sidebar, page 162)

3 tablespoons glutinous rice flour (mochiko; see sidebar, page 139)

1 tablespoon ground chia seeds

1 teaspoon baking powder

½ teaspoon sea salt

¼ cup dry polenta (coarse cornmeal)

3 tablespoons sesame seeds

3 tablespoons sunflower seeds

¼ cup olive oil

½ cup plus 2 tablespoons water

Preheat the oven to 350°F. Combine the brown rice flour, oat flour, glutinous rice flour, chia seeds, baking powder, and salt in a large bowl and use a whisk to mix well. Stir in the polenta, sesame seeds, and sunflower seeds. With a fork, mix in the olive oil and then use your fingers to mix it all together so that the oil permeates the mixture. Finally, mix in the water. The mixture will seem wet at first, but as you mix, it will begin to dry out. Gather it into a ball.

Put the dough on a sheet of parchment paper the size of a half-sheet pan (13 by 18 inches). Pat it out into a rectangle about 1½ inches thick. Place another sheet of parchment paper on top and use a rolling pin to roll the dough out to the size of the pan. Lift the dough by the bottom piece of parchment paper to transfer it to a half-sheet pan and use a knife to cut the dough into cracker-size squares. Bake for about 30 minutes. The crackers will pull away from the sides of the pan and each other and be firm and golden brown. As they cool, they will become crisp. Store in an airtight container for several weeks.

MAKES 1 HALF-SHEET PAN

delicate flax seed crackers

These are the crispest, most delicate gluten-free crackers. You can season them with a variety of herbs and spices and give your own spin to them. My favorite combination of seasonings is 1 tablespoon herbes de Provence and 1 teaspoon white truffle oil. They can be quite addictive. And it's a fabulous way to use up the strained flax seeds from the Flax Seed Egg Whites recipe (page 64).

Strained flax seeds from Flax Seed Egg Whites (page 64)

½ cup almond meal

½ cup water

Sea salt and freshly ground black pepper

Herbs and seasonings

Preheat the oven to 300°F. Line one or two baking sheets with parchment paper and lightly oil the paper. Mix all of the ingredients, including your desired amount of herbs and seasonings, together in a bowl. Spread the mixture thinly on the prepared sheets and bake for about 40 minutes, until crispy. Break apart into large pieces. Store in an airtight container at room temperature for 3 to 4 weeks.

MAKES 1 HALF-SHEET PAN

as you like it crackers

These are simple, basic crackers that can be flavored any way you like and have that artisanal look. Add some herbs, garlic powder, salt and pepper, and a bit of truffle oil, or make them cheesy with some nutritional yeast.

---

2 cups all-purpose flour, or 1 cup all-purpose flour plus 1 cup whole wheat pastry flour

1 teaspoon baking powder

½ teaspoon sea salt

¼ cup olive oil

½ cup water, plus more as needed

Preheat the oven to 350°F. Combine the flour, baking powder, and sea salt in a bowl and mix well. Drizzle in the olive oil and mix with a spoon; some lumps will form, and some of the flour will look like cornmeal. There's no need to break up the lumps, as they will help ensure a flakier cracker. Add the water and mix well to combine; the dough will not be smooth, but will look a little rough. This is fine. If there are patches of dry flour, add up to 2 tablespoons more water as necessary to make it all stick together. Don't overwork it.

Gather it together into a ball and divide it in half. Pat each half into a rectangle about ½ inch thick. Now you'll roll out each half. Put one piece of dough between two sheets of parchment paper and roll it out as thin as you can, almost as large as a half-sheet pan (13 by 18 inches). At this point, if you want uniformly sized crackers, you can cut the rolled-out dough with a sharp knife into squares or rectangles or leave it whole to break into irregular (think artisan!) pieces later. Repeat with the other piece of dough. (If you have a pasta roller, you can use that to roll them out, too.) Bake for 20 to 25 minutes, until the crackers are crisp and golden brown.

Store the crackers in an airtight container for several weeks.

MAKES ALMOST 2 HALF-SHEET PANS

continued ⊃

VARIATIONS

HERB CRACKERS Add about 1 tablespoon of any dried herbs, such as rosemary or thyme, or a combination, such as an Italian blend, to the flour mixture. Add ½ teaspoon of garlic powder as well if you like.

SALT AND PEPPER Spray the top of the rolled-out dough lightly with water or brush with olive oil, then sprinkle with flaked salt, such as Maldon, and coarsely ground pepper.

CHEESY THYME CRACKERS Add 3 tablespoons of nutritional yeast and 1 tablespoon of dried thyme to the flour mixture and stir well.

ROSEMARY GARLIC CRACKERS Before baking, brush the top of the rolled-out dough lightly with olive oil, then sprinkle with rosemary, either fresh or dried, and minced garlic.

focaccia

Herbaceous, crusty, and delicious, this focaccia is perfect with cheese or soup or for savory sandwiches. The top is a bit crustier than traditional focaccia, so if you like a soft crust, brush some soy milk on it before baking.

5 cups all-purpose flour

1 tablespoon dried thyme

1 tablespoon dried marjoram

1 tablespoon dried rosemary

2 teaspoons sea salt

1 teaspoon active dry yeast

2⅓ cups water

⅓ cup olive oil

Combine the dry ingredients in a large bowl. Make a well in the center of the flour mixture, and pour in the water and oil. Mix to make a sticky dough. Cover with a towel and leave it on the counter for 12 to 24 hours.

A couple of hours before you are ready to bake, grease or line a half-sheet pan with parchment paper. Roll or stretch the dough out to cover most of the pan in a uniform thickness. Let it rise for an hour or two until almost doubled. Preheat the oven to 350°F and then bake the focaccia for 40 minutes, until golden brown and crusty on top. If a softer crust is desired, brush the top with soy milk or other nondairy milk before baking and brush again after you pull it out of the oven. Like all breads, focaccia is best enjoyed when freshly baked. To keep it around for a day or two, store it in a paper bag at room temperature. Pop it in the oven for a few minutes to refresh. You can freeze it for a few weeks by putting it in a plastic bag. Be sure to warm it up before serving!

MAKES 1 HALF-SHEET PAN

basic french baguette

I've been making bread since I was a kid, and I've tried just about every technique out there—the standard yeast method, sponge method, sourdough method, natural yeast method, slow-rise method, even the bread maker method. No matter which method, they all required a good several hours in the kitchen devoted to mixing, kneading, and babysitting the multiple risings and final baking. In college, a good friend, to earn a little cash, baked and sold the most amazing baguettes every Friday. They were indeed special, and it was all I could do not to eat the whole loaf in one sitting. To produce this marvel, she had to wake up twice during the night to punch down the dough (this deterred me from asking her for the recipe). A stellar version of the staff of life was a hard-earned prize, it seemed.

But a few years ago, I came across the no-knead method developed by Jim Lahey, and my bread world was turned upside down. While every other approach to bread required the rolling up of sleeves to manipulate the dough on a floured surface or in a mixer, followed by the hours-long doughsitting, Lahey discovered that all you had to do was simply mix the dough, then set it aside for many hours to let the gluten develop itself. There was no need to knead! And no need to hang around—simply mix, then go about your business for 12 to 24 hours, or even days! Since then, I've adapted all of my bread recipes to this new method and saved myself much time and many headaches.

---

5 cups all-purpose or bread flour

2 teaspoons sea salt

½ teaspoon active dry yeast

2¼ cups water

In a large mixing bowl, combine the flour, salt, and yeast. Stir in the water to make a slightly sticky dough. Cover the bowl with a towel and let it proof on the kitchen counter for 12 to 24 hours.

About 1 hour before you're ready to bake, place a pizza stone in the oven and preheat it to 450°F. Turn the dough out onto a floured surface and divide it into two.

continued >

Roll each piece into a thin log about 12 inches long. Cover the dough and let it rise until the pizza stone is nice and hot. Brush the tops of the baguettes with water and gently set them on the stone. Bake for about 30 minutes, until crusty and brown. Baguettes are always best consumed the day you bake them. If you need to keep it for a day or two, store it in a paper bag at room temperature. To refresh, sprinkle a bit of water on it and reheat in the oven for a few minutes until crisp. You can also freeze them for a few weeks by wrapping well in plastic wrap or a plastic bag.

Note: If you start this in the morning and need it by evening—in other words, in 8 to 9 hours—increase the yeast to 1 teaspoon. The longer the dough has to proof, the more character it will have, but it will still be delicious made the expedited way.

MAKES 2 BAGUETTES

pumpkin dinner rolls

These moist, buttery rolls have been a Thanksgiving tradition in my home for over twenty years. When my kids were little, I would have to hide them because they would fill up on the sweet, pillowy balls before the feast even began. Over the years, I've tinkered with the recipe, giving a boost to the pumpkin flavor and applying the "no-knead" principle to it, making it a much easier project to embark on during the busy holiday period.

---

1 cup nondairy milk

1 cup pumpkin puree, canned or homemade

¼ cup maple syrup

⅓ cup Glorious Butterless Butter (page 58), melted

1½ teaspoons sea salt

1 teaspoon yeast

3½ to 4 cups all-purpose flour

In a large bowl, combine the milk, pumpkin, and syrup and whisk together. Add the melted butter and salt and mix again. Sprinkle the yeast over the mixture, then add 3½ cups of the flour and mix thoroughly. If the mixture is moist but not super sticky, don't add any more flour, but if it is very wet and sticky, add the remaining ½ cup flour and mix. Don't knead. Place a towel or piece of plastic wrap over the bowl and let it sit on your counter overnight or up to 24 hours, where it will rise very slowly.

About 2 hours before you are ready to bake, give the dough a stir. It will still be soft, but not sticky. Line two baking sheets with parchment paper. Divide the dough in half, then in half again, then each quarter into six pieces. Roll each piece into a ball and set at least 3 inches apart on the baking sheets. Let the balls rise in a warm corner of the kitchen for about 2 hours. Preheat the oven to 350°F, then bake the rolls for about 20 minutes, until golden brown. Store in a ziplock bag at room temperature for a day or two. Refresh by popping them in the oven for a few minutes.

Note: If you enjoy a soft crust, brush the rolls with a little nondairy milk when they come out of the oven. They will dry quickly.

MAKES 2 DOZEN ROLLS

VARIATION

CLASSIC DINNER ROLLS Omit the pumpkin and increase the soy milk to 1¼ cups. Proceed with the recipe as directed.

basic yeasted sweet pastry dough

Incredibly light and flaky, this dough was inspired by Bo Brink, a Swedish friend from the past. Bo owned a little bakery in San Francisco where I rented space when I first got started baking and selling vegan cakes. Always covered in patches of flour and smelling a bit like day-old Danish, he was as sweet as his confections. Of course, he made his sweet dough the traditional way with lots of eggs and butter, but also with a hint of cardamom, the way it was made back in the old country. This forms the base for anything your imagination can handle, from cinnamon rolls, to Danish pastries, to mock croissants. Fill it, roll it, glaze it as you like, and have that Sunday brunch you've been dreaming of. (This dough can easily be halved if you don't want so much.)

½ cup cashews

2¼ cups soy milk or almond milk

¾ cup Glorious Butterless Butter (page 58), melted

½ cup maple syrup or brown rice syrup (maple is sweeter)

1½ teaspoons active dry yeast

2 teaspoon salt

1½ teaspoons ground cardamom

5½ to 6 cups all-purpose flour (not bread flour)

In a blender, process the cashews and about half of the soy milk (you needn't be exact) until smooth and creamy. Pour this into a large bowl and add the remaining soy milk. Add the butter, maple syrup, yeast, salt, and cardamom and mix well. Finally, mix in the flour. The dough will be very sticky. You will need to add a bit more or less, depending on a variety of factors, including humidity, water content of the flour, and how much it has settled in the bag. You are looking for a sticky but not wet dough, much stickier than traditional bread dough. As it proofs by itself, the gluten will develop and the dough will become less sticky. Again, there is no need to knead the dough. As it proofs slowly, the gluten will develop and "knead" itself.

Cover the bowl with a towel and let it sit at room temperature overnight, until doubled in size and somewhat airy looking. This could take anywhere from 8 to 12 hours, depending on the temperature of the room. If you want to make the dough a couple of days ahead of baking, put the dough in a large bowl, cover it

continued >

◁ basic yeasted sweet pastry dough, continued

with plastic wrap, and let it proof in the refrigerator for 24 to 48 hours (it will proof slower due to the lower temperature). If you choose to proof the dough in the refrigerator, you will need to pull it out and let it come to room temperature 1 to 3 hours before using.

When you are ready to bake, gently scrape the dough out of the bowl onto a floured surface. Now follow the directions that follow on page 183 to shape, fill, and bake, or use a favorite recipe from another source for shaping, filling, and baking.

MAKES ABOUT 3 POUNDS, ENOUGH FOR 18 TO 24 AVERAGE-SIZE PASTRIES

HOW TO USE BASIC YEASTED SWEET PASTRY DOUGH

If you're making any of the following recipes in a cold climate, or if your house is really cold, you can increase the yeast by 1 teaspoon.

cinnamon rolls

Preheat the oven 350°F. Line a baking sheet with parchment paper. Divide the dough into two pieces, handling it as gently as possible (don't punch down or knead!). Roll each one into an 8 by 10-inch rectangle about ½ inch thick. Sprinkle the surface with organic sugar, coconut sugar, or brown rice syrup and generously sprinkle with cinnamon. If you like, you can add raisins, chopped walnuts, or pecans. Roll up tightly and cut into ten pieces. Arrange them on the baking sheet about ½ inch apart. It's best to let them proof at room temperature for an hour for the fluffiest texture, but you can bake them right away as well and they should still get a good rise. Bake for about 25 minutes, until puffy and golden brown.

sticky fingers (a less sweet version than the usual)

Preheat the oven to 350°F. Grease two cake pans. Divide the dough into two pieces, handling the dough as gently as possible, and roll each one into an 8 by 10-inch rectangle about ½ inch thick. Sprinkle the surface with brown rice syrup and pecans. Put the rolls in the pans ½ inch apart, then pour more brown rice syrup and pecans on top. Of course, you can melt some Glorious Butterless Butter (page 58) and pour some of that on top as well. Bake for 25 to 30 minutes, until golden brown.

danish pastries

You can make pastries with any filling. Jams, jellies, vegan cream cheese, marzipan, or finely chopped nuts mixed with maple syrup and cinnamon are all great fillings. Preheat the oven 350°F. Line a baking sheet with parchment paper. To fill and shape, divide the dough in two, handling it as gently as possible. Roll out each half into a 6 by 12-inch rectangle. Put a row of filling down the middle and then fold both sides over to meet in the middle. Cut the folded dough crosswise into slices about 2 inches wide and set the slices a couple of inches apart on the baking sheet. Cut a slit down the middle of each top and separate it slightly. Bake for about 25 minutes, until golden brown.

easy refrigerated pizza dough

The trick to crisp but chewy pizza crust is not letting the dough rise until it hits a hot oven. And that oven should be hot—as high as your oven will go. A pizza stone really amps up the score, helping yield that crunchy bottom.

---

4 cups bread flour

2 teaspoons sea salt

1 teaspoon active dry yeast

2 cups cold water

Mix all the ingredients in a large bowl to make a sticky dough. Cover with plastic wrap or put it into a plastic bag and keep it in the refrigerator for 1 to 3 days. About an hour before you're ready to eat, turn on the oven as high as it will go, preferably 500°F. Put your pizza stone in it and let it get good and hot for 1 hour (if you don't have one, use a cast-iron pan). During that time, prep your ingredients—veggies, vegan pepperoni (page 126), sauce, cheese. Right before you're ready to bake, divide the dough in two and roll one half out on a lightly floured pizza peel (or shape it by tossing in the air if you can!). Put your toppings on it, slide it onto the hot stone, and bake for about 10 minutes. Repeat with the remaining dough.

MAKES 2 PIZZA CRUSTS

quick cornmeal pizza crust

With a bit of crunch from the cornmeal, this makes a good crust when you want pizza in a hurry. Best when rolled out thin so that it bubbles up in spots like yeasted dough, it's still tasty even when it's thicker. From mixing to finale is about 1 hour, so you can make it on a weeknight. This one is particularly good as a "salad pizza," topped with a pile of freshly tossed mixed greens. You can also bake it plain and turn it into crackers.

2 cups cornmeal

1½ cups all-purpose flour

1 tablespoon baking powder

1½ teaspoons sea salt

⅓ cup olive oil

1 cup water

Place a pizza stone or cast-iron skillet in the oven and preheat it to 450°F. Leave the pizza stone or skillet in there for at least 45 minutes while preparing the dough, sauce, and toppings.

Combine the cornmeal, flour, baking powder, and salt in a large bowl and whisk to combine well. Pour in the olive oil and water and mix well. Turn out onto a lightly floured board and knead for 1 to 2 minutes, until the dough is smooth and pliable.

Divide the dough in two and roll it out on a lightly floured pizza peel into a 10- to 12-inch circle. If you can get it to just under ⅛ inch, it will get very crispy and light and will bubble in places. Now cover with whatever sauce and toppings you like and slide it off of the peel onto the stone or skillet. Bake for about 15 minutes, until the bottom is brown and crisp.

MAKES 2 PIZZA CRUSTS

VARIATION

GLUTEN-FREE CORNMEAL CRUST Instead of all-purpose flour, substitute oat flour (see sidebar, page 162) or a commercial gluten-free flour and add 1 tablespoon xanthan gum. If the mixture seems too wet to roll out, add an extra ¼ cup oat or gluten-free flour (different flour mixes have variable absorption rates, requiring a bit more or less).

sweet endings

A happy, sweet ending to every story—that's what we all want. But when it comes to food, many of us crave that sweetness in the beginning, middle, and end, indulging a bit too much. If only our bodies responded as sweetly to the consumption of desserts as our souls do. They don't, especially as we get older, so it's best to practice moderation. (I'm smiling as I say this.) In Japan, dessert is often just a piece of fruit, and that is how it should be most of the time. But I'm like everyone else, and I don't pretend not to enjoy a special dessert once in a while. So when I do enjoy them, I want them to be extra special. I want every bite to be worth it.

My approach to dessert is not to compromise flavor. Where I've found it possible to balance flavor with health, I do, and I offer low-fat or fruit-sweetened options (check out the oat-based gelatos, pages 211 and 212, or the fruit-only sorbet, page 213). But the majority of recipes here take a more traditional approach to desserts, using organic sugar, maple syrup, or coconut sugar. In some cases, you can opt to use xylitol or erythritol, natural sugars that have fewer or no calories and don't affect blood sugar levels as much or at all.

As in the rest of the book, what you'll find in this chapter are the foundations—cake mixes that will make your life easy when you want to bake brownies, cookies, or cake in a jiffy; spectacular buttercreams and icings that can be frozen for months and used when necessary; lemon curd, custard, and pastry cream to fill all of your creations; basic formulas for ice cream, sorbet, and gelato that let you customize your own flavors; and old, perhaps forgotten, regulars like condensed milk and white chocolate that fill in for their dairy counterparts in your favorite recipes. Whatever your sweet fantasy, you can make it come to life using the components you'll find here.

white cake and baking mix

Capture that "made from scratch" flavor almost instantly with this mix.

8 cups all-purpose flour

3 cups organic sugar

⅔ cup almond meal

6 tablespoons ground flax seeds

6 tablespoons baking powder

1 teaspoon sea salt

In a large bowl, combine all of the ingredients and stir with a whisk for about 1 minute, until everything is evenly distributed. Alternatively, you can use an electric mixer or a food processor, if you have a big one where it will all fit. You can store this in a sealed container or ziplock bags in the pantry for several months.

MAKES ABOUT 12 CUPS

HOW TO USE WHITE CAKE AND BAKING MIX

oil-free lemon blueberry or cherry muffins

Having muffins for breakfast without getting up super early is now a reality!

1 cup nondairy milk

¾ cup applesauce

2 teaspoons lemon zest

2½ cups White Cake and Baking Mix

1 cup blueberries or pitted cherries, either fresh or frozen

Preheat the oven to 400°F. Grease the cups of a 12-cup muffin tin. In a bowl, whisk together the milk, applesauce, and lemon zest. Add the cake mix and stir only to combine—it should be lumpy to provide a quick, light rise. Mix in the fruit gently, being sure not to overmix. Spoon into your muffin tin and bake for 15 to 20 minutes, until beautiful peaks form and they are golden brown.

MAKES 12 MUFFINS

VARIATION

CHOCOLATE CHIP MUFFINS Omit the lemon zest and substitute 1 cup chocolate chips for the blueberries or cherries.

classic white cake

Unbelievably light and fluffy in both texture and flavor without being overly sweet, this makes the perfect birthday cake. It also holds up to a bit of soaking, so if you like, dab the top with a favorite liqueur or syrup. You can layer and frost it with French Buttercream (page 195) or French Chocolate Buttercream (page 196). (Pictured on page 194.)

3¾ cups White Cake and Baking Mix (page 188)

3 cups nondairy milk, preferably warm

¾ cup canola or other neutral oil

1 tablespoon apple cider vinegar

1 tablespoon vanilla extract

Preheat the oven to 350°F. Grease two 9-inch cake pans and line the bottoms with parchment paper. Put the cake mix into a large bowl and make a well in the center. Add the milk, oil, vinegar, and vanilla and, using a whisk or electric mixer, whisk or mix gently for about 30 seconds, until smooth (contrary to the popular belief about not overmixing, cake batters should be mixed thoroughly to ensure even rising and small air pockets). Pour into the cake pans and bake for about 20 minutes, until springy and a knife inserted into the center comes out clean.

MAKES TWO 9-INCH CAKE LAYERS

peanut butter cookies

These light, crisp, perfect cookies practically melt in your mouth.

4 ounces (about ½ cup) Glorious Butterless Butter (page 58), at room temperature

1 cup peanut butter

¼ cup maple syrup

1½ cups White Cake and Baking Mix (page 188)

Preheat the oven to 350°F. Line a baking sheet with parchment paper. In the bowl of a stand mixer or in a large bowl using a wooden spoon, cream the butter until smooth, add the peanut butter and syrup, and mix. Stir in the cake mix. Form into balls, place on the baking sheet a couple of inches apart, and use the tines of a fork to flatten them out. Bake for 10 minutes. They are very fragile while warm, so even if you are tempted, resist until they cool completely!

MAKES 24 COOKIES

chocolate cake and baking mix

With this in the pantry, you'll have no reason to deny yourself a chocolate fix when the mood strikes. If you're looking for that perfect chocolate cake—rich, complex, but light—look no further. How about deep, fudgy brownies (pictured opposite)? It's right here. Or almost guilt-free and oil-free chocolate muffins? Got those covered, too. Best of all, if you have kids like mine who tell you at ten o'clock at night that they need a treat to take to school the next day, you'll be the supermom who can whip out amazing desserts "from scratch" in moments.

3 cups whole wheat pastry flour

3 cups unbleached flour

4½ cups coconut sugar, or 4 cups organic sugar

1½ cups cocoa powder (not Dutch-processed)

6 tablespoons very finely ground coffee (espresso grind)

2 tablespoons baking soda

1 tablespoon ground cinnamon

1 tablespoon sea salt

Sift together all of the ingredients into a large bowl, then using a wire whisk, mix well until the mixture looks perfectly combined. Alternatively, you can use an electric mixer or food processor. Store in an airtight container or ziplock bags at room temperature for 3 to 4 months.

MAKES 12 CUPS

continued ⋗

HOW TO USE CHOCOLATE CAKE AND BAKING MIX

classic brownies

This is the kind of brownie that is crackled on top, with a dark, fudgy center, deep in buttery flavor, and totally satisfying. (Pictured on page 191.)

6 ounces dark chocolate

½ cup Glorious Butterless Butter (page 58)

1 tablespoon ground chia seeds

3 tablespoons water

2 cups Chocolate Cake and Baking Mix (page 190)

¼ cup maple syrup

½ cup chopped walnuts or pecans (optional)

Preheat the oven to 350°F. Line an 8-inch square baking pan with parchment paper and grease the sides. In a double boiler, melt the chocolate and butter together. In a small bowl, mix together the chia seeds and water. Put the cake mix in a large bowl and make a well in the center. Pour in the melted chocolate mixture, chia seed mixture, and syrup and mix well. Stir in the nuts. Pour the mixture into the pan. Bake for 20 minutes. It will look dry on top but will still be soft inside. Allow it to cool completely before cutting and serving.

MAKES ABOUT 16 BROWNIES

classic chocolate cake

Ever so light and delicate, sandwich these layers together with French Buttercream (page 195) or French Chocolate Buttercream (page 196).

4 cups (12 ounces) Chocolate Cake and Baking Mix (page 190)

2 cups boiling water

½ cup oil

2 tablespoons apple cider vinegar

2 teaspoons vanilla extract

Preheat the oven to 350°F. Line two cake pans with parchment paper and grease or spray the sides with a light coating of oil or line a 12-cup muffin tin with paper liners. Put the mix in a medium bowl. In a separate medium bowl, combine the boiling water with the oil, vinegar, and vanilla and pour it into the cake mix in the bowl. Whisk for at least 30 seconds. Pour the mixture into the pans or cups and bake for 15 to 20 minutes, until the middle is springy to the touch.

MAKES TWO 9-INCH ROUND OR 8-INCH SQUARE CAKE LAYERS, OR 12 CUPCAKES

oil-free chocolate muffins or cupcakes

These are surprisingly moist and tender. You'll never miss the oil!

1½ cups nondairy milk

½ cup mashed very ripe banana
(about 1 small) or applesauce

2 teaspoons apple cider vinegar

2½ cups Chocolate Cake and Baking Mix
(page 190)

¾ cup chocolate chips (optional)

Grease the cups of a 12-cup muffin tin or line with paper liners. In a bowl, whisk together the milk, banana, and vinegar. Add the cake mix and whisk quickly to combine. Stir in the chocolate chips. Pour into the prepared muffin tin and bake for 20 to 25 minutes, until springy.

MAKES 12 MUFFINS OR CUPCAKES

double chocolate chip cookies

Get a double dose of chocolate right here!

½ cup Glorious Butterless Butter
(page 58)

¼ cup maple syrup

1 tablespoon ground chia seeds

2 tablespoons water

2 cups Chocolate Cake and Baking Mix
(page 190)

1 teaspoon vanilla extract

¾ cup chocolate chips

Preheat the oven to 350°F. Line two baking sheets with parchment paper. Cream the butter and syrup together in a medium bowl. In a small bowl, mix the chia seeds and water, and add to the butter mixture. Stir in the cake mix and vanilla, then add the chocolate chips. Drop by spoonfuls onto the baking sheets about 2 inches apart. Bake for about 10 minutes, until the tops are dry to the touch. Let them cool on the sheet for a bit before transferring to a cooling rack, as they are quite fragile when warm.

MAKES 18 TO 24 COOKIES

french buttercream

In college, I had a good friend who moonlighted as a caterer. She let me help her from time to time and forever spoiled me with her Kirsch torte. I remember to this day the first time I took a bite of the lovely, light génoise layers soaked in Kirsch, adorned with a rich, fluffy, melt-in-your-mouth buttercream that was unlike any of the sugary frostings I had known. I was happy to receive payment in slices of this heavenly cake.

This buttercream is my dedication to Kirsch torte. Divinely light, with none of that cloyingly sweet and greasy sensation that coats your tongue and throat, this is the vegan answer to decorating glorious cakes. You can flavor this as you like with a shot of your favorite liqueur, such as Kirsch or Grand Marnier, or a few drops of a favorite extract. And what should you layer it with? Why, of course, look to the Classic White Cake (page 188) or Classic Chocolate Cake (page 190) as your answer!

---

1 cup water

½ cup cashews

½ cup organic sugar

1 cup oil

4 ounces cocoa butter, melted

8 ounces unsalted Glorious Butterless Butter (page 58)

1 tablespoon vanilla extract

2 tablespoons Grand Marnier, Kirschwasser, Frangelico, rum, or other liqueur (optional)

In a blender, combine the water, cashews, and sugar and blend until creamy and smooth. Add the oil and melted cocoa butter and blend again to emulsify to a creamy consistency. Transfer the mixture to a bowl and let it chill in the refrigerator for at least 2 to 3 hours; it will firm up a bit. Using an electric mixer, whip in the butter a tablespoon or two at a time until light, fluffy, and increased in volume by 30 to 50 percent. Finally, add the vanilla and liqueur and mix to blend. If it does not whip up and become fluffy, it is not cold enough; put it back in the refrigerator for 2 to 3 hours, then rewhip until you have mounds of fluffy buttercream.

Use right away to decorate your layers or refrigerate for up to 2 weeks. Rewhip it before using. You can also freeze it for 3 to 4 months.

MAKES 5 TO 6 CUPS AFTER WHIPPING, ENOUGH TO FILL AND FROST 2 TWO-LAYER 8- OR 9-INCH CAKES

french chocolate buttercream

In high school, I spent evenings poring over the pages of my parents'
Time-Life Good Cook series. In one of them, I discovered the Dobos
torte—a multilayered concoction of thin, slightly crisp cake layers
sandwiched by an ethereal chocolate buttercream. I devoured the bowlful
of frosting and had almost nothing left for the cake.

As in the preceding French Buttercream recipe, this is not based on
powdered sugar and shortening. I have borrowed cues from the classic
way of making buttercream with custard and butter, and applied them to
vegan ingredients to create a chocolate buttercream that I think is worthy
of a Dobos torte. As one tester said, she also almost ate the whole bowlful.

This is not a last-minute frosting; the mixture needs to chill for several
hours before whipping. However, it can be made ahead and frozen for
months, and then thawed and whipped to a delightfully airy consistency
when you're ready to use it.

½ cup cashews, soaked in water for
3 to 8 hours, drained and rinsed

1¼ cups canola oil

¼ cup water

12 ounces silken tofu

12 ounces dark or semisweet chocolate,
melted (see sidebar)

4 ounces unsweetened chocolate (aka
chocolate liquor), melted (see sidebar)

3 tablespoons maple syrup or organic sugar

1 tablespoon vanilla extract

1 to 2 tablespoons brandy, rum, or Grand
Marnier (optional)

In a high-speed blender, combine the cashews, oil, and water on high speed until
absolutely smooth and creamy. Add the tofu, both kinds of melted chocolate, syrup,
vanilla, and alcohol and blend again until the mixture is completely smooth and
creamy. Pour this mixture, which will be warm, into a metal bowl or shallow dish
and chill in the refrigerator for several hours, until cold and somewhat solidified.
Transfer to an electric mixer (or into a large bowl and use a handheld electric mixer)
and whip for 7 to 8 minutes, until light and fluffy. It will increase in volume while
becoming lighter in color and texture.

If you are not going to ice a cake right away, store the buttercream in a covered container in the refrigerator and rewhip it before using so that it's easily spreadable. Use it to sandwich any of the cakes or brownies made with White Cake and Baking Mix (page 188) or Chocolate Cake and Baking Mix (page 190).

MAKES 6½ CUPS, ENOUGH TO FILL AND FROST 2 TWO-LAYER 8- OR 9-INCH CAKES

VARIATIONS

MOCHA BUTTERCREAM In place of water, use ⅓ cup espresso or very strong coffee. Alternatively, you can use 1 tablespoon instant coffee, dissolved in 1 tablespoon hot water. If desired, add 2 tablespoons Kahlúa or other coffee liqueur.

SWEETER CHOCOLATE BUTTERCREAM If a sweeter buttercream is to your liking, use semisweet chocolate to replace both the bittersweet and the unsweetened chocolate.

HOW TO MELT CHOCOLATE PROPERLY

Chocolate can be melted either on the stove top or in the microwave. Either way, the chocolate should never be allowed to get hot. Imagine a bar of chocolate melting on the dashboard of your car on a summer day—chocolate melts at about 85°F, so it never needs to feel warm or hot. You also want to make sure that the bowl you use is absolutely dry—even a drop of water can render a grainy chocolate.

To melt in a microwave: If necessary, chop the chocolate on a dry cutting board into chunks. Combine the chocolates in a dry glass bowl and microwave for 1 minute. Remove, stir with a wooden spoon, and return to the microwave for another 30 seconds. Again, remove, stir, and repeat if necessary. As you stir, the chocolate will melt. Repeat this until it is completely melted.

To melt on the stove: Place the chocolates in a dry glass or metal bowl, or in the top of a double boiler. If you do not have a double boiler, place the bowl over a pot with a smaller diameter that has about 1 inch of water in it. Bring the water to a simmer and begin to stir the chocolate with a wooden spoon. When it begins to melt, turn off the heat and continue stirring until completely melted, making sure that it never gets hot to the touch.

lemon curd

This classic, zesty filling captures the essence of lemons, beautifully balanced with creamy richness. It's the perfect foil for tarts, lemon bars, parfaits, and, of course, lemon cream pie.

1 cup water

1 cup cashews, soaked in water for 3 to 8 hours, drained and rinsed

1 cup organic sugar

¾ cup freshly squeezed lemon juice

Zest of 5 lemons (about 2 tablespoons)

½ cup unsalted or low-salt Glorious Butterless Butter (page 58)

Pinch of turmeric or natural yellow food coloring (optional)

In a blender, combine the water and cashews and process until very smooth and creamy. Pour this mixture into a saucepan and bring it to a simmer, stirring almost constantly with a rubber spatula to ensure that it doesn't burn on the bottom. The mixture will thicken and should be smooth; if it begins to get clumpy, use a whisk to smooth it out. When thick, add the sugar, lemon juice, and lemon zest and cook for a few more minutes until creamy. Remove the pan from the heat.

Whisk in the butter by the tablespoon until fully incorporated. The mixture will be ivory in color, so if you prefer a lemony color, whisk in a pinch of turmeric or food coloring to achieve the desired color. Pour the mixture into a jar or container with a lid and let it cool completely in the refrigerator before using. It will thicken as it cools. Store the lemon curd in an airtight container for up to 1 week in the refrigerator or several months in the freezer.

MAKES ABOUT 2 CUPS

HOW TO USE LEMON CURD

Lemon curd can be served on top of or alongside pound cake, scones, or biscuits. Use it as a spread for toast or waffles. Make parfaits by alternating layers of lemon curd, Better Than Whipping Cream and Topping (page 79), and fruit. Fill a baked pie shell with it, top it with Better Than Whipping Cream and Topping (page 79) or Flax Seed Meringue (page 67), and serve it as lemon cream or lemon meringue pie. Or feature it in the Lemon Bars recipe below.

lemon bars

Zesty lemon curd baked atop a delicate shortbread is a recipe for success!

¾ cup pastry flour

3 tablespoons rice flour

Pinch of salt

4 ounces Glorious Butterless Butter (page 58), cut into pieces

¼ cup organic sugar

About 1⅓ cups Lemon Curd (page 198)

Preheat the oven to 350°F. In a food processor, combine the flours and salt and process for a few seconds. Add the butter and sugar, and process briefly until combined. Pat into an 8 by 8-inch baking pan and pour the lemon curd on top. Bake for 25 to 30 minutes. Let cool completely, then refrigerate for a couple of hours to help it set. Cut into bars and serve.

MAKES ABOUT 16 BARS

custard

Custard can take many forms, from crème anglaise to flan. In the United States, custard is often a light pudding that is used to fill pies, top cakes, or just eat with a spoon. My version has a refined texture and delicate flavor that can be modified as desired.

1 (13.5-ounce) can low-fat coconut milk

⅓ cup maple syrup or organic sugar (maple imparts a nice flavor, but sugar makes a whiter custard)

1 vanilla bean, split, or 2 teaspoons vanilla extract

2 tablespoons Glorious Butterless Butter (page 58)

1 tablespoon brandy (optional)

3 tablespoons cornstarch

3 tablespoons water

Combine the coconut milk, syrup, vanilla, and butter in a saucepan over medium low heat and bring it all to a simmer. Add the brandy. In a small bowl, dissolve the cornstarch in the water and whisk it into the custard until it thickens and becomes glossy. This should take only moments; do not overcook, or it may become rubbery. If you have used a vanilla bean, take it out at this time. Pour the mixture into a bowl, cover, and refrigerate for several hours, until thick. To soften before using, stir with a whisk. Store the custard in an airtight container for up to 1 week in the refrigerator or several months in the freezer.

MAKES ABOUT 2½ CUPS

VARIATIONS

PASTRY CREAM One of the things I most missed when I went vegan was crème pâtissière, or pastry cream, the versatile base for filling fruit tarts, Napoleons, Danish, and so many other wonderful little things. To make pastry cream, increase the corn-starch to ¼ cup. When the custard is cool, fold 1 cup Better Than Whipping Cream and Topping (page 79) into it. Alternatively, you can fold in coconut whipped cream (refrigerate a can of full-fat coconut milk for several days, then spoon out the thickened and separated cream, reserving the remaining liquid for another purpose. Whip the thickened cream until stiff). Makes 3½ cups.

COFFEE PASTRY CREAM Substitute ¼ cup espresso for ¼ cup of the coconut milk. Makes 3½ cups.

HOW TO USE CUSTARD OR PASTRY CREAM

Custard can serve in a variety of lead and supporting roles. Banana cream pie? Use this custard as the base. How about trifle? Mix this custard with leftover cake crumbs and fruit. You'll find countless uses for this in your dessert repertoire. While light and fluffy, pastry cream makes a very stable filling for all sorts of pastries. It is the key to perfect fresh fruit tarts—bake a pie crust blind (without filling), let cool, then brush a little melted apricot jam on the bottom. Fill with pastry cream, top with fresh fruit (such as berries, mangoes, grapes, kiwi), and glaze with a bit more melted jam for a shine. Or try it as a filling for crepes (try the buckwheat crepes, page 163) with fruit or compote. Or best of all, give the Éclairs recipe below a whirl.

éclairs

Classic éclairs filled with pastry cream and glazed in chocolate seem to be made from magic. In reality, the unique characteristics of choux pastry—crispy on the outside, puffy and hollow on the inside—happens when an egg-and-flour dough hits the hot oven and it poofs. Of all the veganized versions of traditional recipes I have created over the years, I can honestly say that this was the hardest—it took me over thirty attempts to get it right. And yes, they are a bit fussy to make, as you'll have to have Flax Seed Egg Whites, Glorious Butterless Butter, and the Pastry Cream for it to come together. But are they worth the trouble? If I had to pick a favorite dessert, these might just fill that role.

1 cup soy milk or almond milk

¼ cup Glorious Butterless Butter (page 58)

1 tablespoon organic sugar

Large pinch of salt

1 cup all-purpose flour

⅓ cup water

3 tablespoons store-bought Ener-G Egg Replacer

½ cup Flax Seed Egg Whites (page 64)

1 tablespoon baking powder

2 teaspoons apple cider vinegar

2½ to 3 cups Custard or Pastry Cream (page 200)

3 ounces dark chocolate, melted (see sidebar, page 197)

continued >

Preheat the oven to 400°F. Line two baking sheets with parchment paper. Combine the milk, butter, sugar, and salt in a medium saucepan and bring to a boil over medium-high heat. Turn down the heat a bit, and add the flour all at once, stirring with a wooden spoon to combine, and cook for about 1 minute, until smooth and glossy and a ball forms in the middle of the pan. Remove from the heat and let the mixture cool for a few minutes while preparing the other ingredients.

In a small bowl, combine the water with the egg replacer and beat with a whisk until very thick and frothy. In a food processor, combine the egg replacer mixture, flax egg whites, baking powder, and vinegar. Process for a few seconds, then add the dough from the saucepan and process for about 30 seconds, until the mixture is smooth and pulls away from the sides.

Put this mixture into a pastry bag fitted with a large round tip. Pipe 3-inch-long logs onto the prepared baking sheets. Bake for about 20 minutes, until puffed, golden brown, and almost doubled in size. Because there are slight variations between different ovens, it's a good idea to take one out and split it open with a sharp knife to make sure that it is hollow inside. It's okay if it is slightly moist inside, but it shouldn't be filled with uncooked pastry. If it is, keep baking for a few more minutes. Turn off the oven and allow them to sit in there for another 5 to 10 minutes. Remove them from the oven, and let them cool completely on the pans. Using a sharp knife, split the éclairs in half; the inside should be hollow. If necessary, use a spoon to scrape away any uncooked dough. Fill with the pastry cream—you can do this with a spoon, or more efficiently with a pastry bag. Spread melted chocolate on the tops.

MAKES 16 ÉCLAIRS

homemade vanilla extract

The first time I made my own homemade vanilla extract, I simply couldn't believe it. Not only was it mindlessly easy, but it also cost a tenth of what I was spending on little bottles of high-end vanilla extract. It also solved the problem of what to do with those half-empty bottles of booze left over from last year's holiday party, which cleared out some pantry space. The hardest part was combing the Web for the best deals on quality vanilla beans. For the purpose of making your own vanilla extract, you can use the cosmetically less attractive grade B vanilla pods, which are far less expensive.

The beauty of homemade vanilla extract is that as a bonus, the liquor-soaked beans can be pureed into a fragrant vanilla paste that does wonders in baked goods. That's real bang for your buck!

Homemade vanilla makes a great gift, and no one will believe that you made it.

---

1 cup vodka, rum, or brandy   **8 to 10 vanilla beans**

Pour the liquor into a 2-cup or larger jar. Cut the beans into 1-inch lengths. Put them in the jar. Secure the jar with a lid, then set in a dark place, such as a pantry or closet. Then forget about it for a couple of months or more. Go have a party and squirrel away some more liquor for your next batch. When you remember that you had that vanilla in the pantry, it'll be ready.

Strain through a sieve into a bottle of your choice and store it in your pantry for a year or more. Use the strained vanilla beans to make Vanilla Paste (below).

Note: I usually make about 4 cups at a time, as it takes a few months for it to become "vanilla." You can easily double, triple, or quadruple the quantities.

MAKES 1 CUP

> ### BONUS RECIPE
> VANILLA PASTE Put the soaked, drained vanilla beans into a food processor or blender. Add 2 to 3 tablespoons of organic sugar and process until a thick paste is formed. Pack into a jar and store at room temperature for several months. Use in lieu of vanilla extract.

caramel sauce

Brown rice syrup has a caramel-like flavor and makes the perfect base for a caramel sauce that is not overly sweet. You can use either Cashew Cream (page 56) for a more neutral flavor or coconut milk for a hint of coconut. The Glorious Butterless Butter (page 58) stirred in at the end is an optional enrichment, depending on how indulgent you want to get.

1 cup brown rice syrup

½ cup organic sugar

1 cup Cashew Cream (page 56) or canned coconut milk

1 vanilla bean, split

¼ cup Glorious Butterless Butter (page 58, optional)

Combine the syrup and sugar in a 2-quart pot (it's best to have a good-size pot, as the mixture can boil over if you're not careful). Bring this to a boil over medium heat and simmer, stirring frequently, for 5 to 8 minutes, until it has reduced and is a thick, brown, foaming mass, or it has reached 230°F on a candy thermometer. Also, when the spoon is pulled out, the sauce on it will harden quickly. This is the caramelization process, and how well you do this will determine whether it tastes like caramel. If you don't fully caramelize it, you'll still end up with a tasty vanilla sauce, so fret not.

Whisk in the cashew cream and the vanilla bean, and continue to let it bubble away, stirring frequently, for another 5 to 6 minutes. It should have a bit of viscosity to it but will be thinner than what you might associate with caramel sauce (don't worry; it will thicken as it cools down). Now, if you want it richer, stir in the butter to melt. Remove the vanilla bean. Store in a jar in the refrigerator for several months. To use, place the jar in a pot of hot water to heat and soften the sauce.

MAKES 2 CUPS

HOW TO USE CARAMEL SAUCE

Pour caramel sauce over warm brownies, apple pie, or ice cream or melt with chocolate (see sidebar, page 197) to make a dipping sauce for bananas and other fruit. You can also fold it into whipped coconut cream (see Variations, page 200) as a delicious topping for pies and tarts.

white chocolate

While many scoff at white chocolate because it doesn't actually contain any chocolate, I've always loved its subtle flavor. This version makes creamy, luscious bars for munching or to use in desserts. I highly recommend pulverizing sugar in a blender to make powdered sugar in order to avoid the starchy mouthfeel of commercial varieties that contain cornstarch.

---

4 ounces cocoa butter

½ cup organic sugar

⅓ cup Cashew Cream (page 56)
or soy milk

1 teaspoon vanilla extract

1 teaspoon liquid lecithin (see sidebar,
page 58)

Melt the cocoa butter in a double boiler over medium heat. Pulverize the sugar in a blender until powdered and add it to the melted cocoa butter. Stir until the sugar is fully dissolved. Combine the cashew cream, cocoa butter mixture, vanilla, and lecithin in a blender or food processor and process until fully emulsified. Pour into silicone molds and refrigerate for 24 hours or longer until it is firm. Be patient, as sometimes it takes a couple of days for it to completely firm up into a bar. Wrapped in plastic or wax paper, or stored in a covered container, white chocolate will keep in the refrigerator for 3 to 4 weeks. To store for several months, put it in the freezer.

MAKES ABOUT 10 OUNCES

condensed nondairy milk

The return of condensed milk! When I started writing this book, I reached out to readers and friends asking what staples they'd like to see veganized. I was surprised to find condensed milk mentioned again and again. Having approached desserts from a more European angle in my pre-vegan days, I had limited experience with condensed milk–based desserts. But I concocted a recipe and was delighted that it met with approval from testers who used it to re-create long-forgotten desserts. Yes, it's rich and sweet and works great in Thai iced tea, flan, seven-layer bars, or anything else you might have learned from your grandmother.

2 cups soy milk

1 cup organic sugar

¼ cup refined coconut oil

¼ cup coconut cream (see sidebar)

Combine the milk and sugar in a medium saucepan and bring it to a boil over medium-high heat until reduced by more than half and the mixture is fairly thick. Whisk in the oil and cream and continue cooking until the mixture has reduced to 1 cup. This will keep in a covered container in the refrigerator for 2 to 3 weeks, or you can freeze it for several months.

MAKES 1 CUP

COCONUT CREAM

For coconut cream, refrigerate a can of coconut milk for several days. Open the can and scoop out the thickened cream on the top. Don't discard the remaining liquid, however! Add it to soups, curries, smoothies, or even use as a base for salad dressings.

basic ice cream base

Here's a base for making rich, creamy ice cream—any flavor you want. In the variations, you'll see how to mix it up (Mint Chocolate Chip is pictured here). The combination of cashews and coconut milk creates a neutral base that's not overly nutty or coconutty, making it perfect for flavoring as you like.

1 cup cashews

1½ cups water

1 (13.5-ounce) can full-fat coconut milk

½ to ¾ cup organic sugar

Combine the cashews and water in a blender and process until creamy. Add the coconut milk and ½ cup sugar (or more, depending on desired sweetness), and blend again briefly. Chill until very cold, then pour it into your ice cream maker and process according to the manufacturer's instructions.

To flavor the ice cream, follow the variations on page 210, keeping in mind that the total quantity for the mixture should be no more than 3½ to 4 cups. If you add a liquid item such as coffee or pureed fruit, you should reduce the amount of water in your base accordingly. Don't worry; it's not an exact science, but keeping the total blended mixture at or below 4 cups (not including last-minute add-ins such as chocolate chips, chunks of fruit, and so on) will ensure ultimate creaminess and richness. If it gets too diluted, you run the risk of an icier ice cream. All of the flavors of ice cream will keep in the freezer for 2 to 3 months.

MAKES 4 CUPS

SWEETENING OPTIONS

Adjust the sweetener to your liking, substituting coconut sugar, maple syrup, or even ripe bananas for the sugar. Xylitol or erythritol are low- or no-calorie options that work for this ice cream. Xylitol is derived from birch trees, is lower in calories than sugar, and apparently doesn't cause cavities. Erythritol is a sugar alcohol derived from plants (it occurs naturally in many fruits, including apples) that simply passes through your system and therefore has no calories. However, in large quantities, both of them can cause diarrhea, so be forewarned.

continued ⌐

VARIATIONS

VANILLA Add 1 tablespoon good-quality vanilla extract or scrape out the seeds from 2 vanilla bean pods and process with the cashews.

GREEN TEA Add 3 tablespoons matcha powder to the cashews and water mixture and blend until smooth.

MATCHA MANGO Make the Green Tea Ice Cream above, but toward the end of churning, mix in 1½ cups of diced mangoes. A very refreshing addition!

LIGHT CHOCOLATE Add ½ cup cocoa powder to the mixture in the blender.

DARK, RICH CHOCOLATE Add ½ cup cocoa powder and 8 ounces melted dark chocolate (see sidebar, page 197) to the blender during the final blending.

CAPPUCCINO Replace ½ cup of the water with ½ cup espresso or very strong coffee. Or you can just dissolve a couple of tablespoons of instant coffee in the water.

STRAWBERRY, RASPBERRY, BLUEBERRY, OR MANGO Blend 2 cups of fruit chunks (10 to 12 ounces) with the coconut milk in a blender until smooth. Add the cashews and only ½ cup water, and process again until smooth.

MINT CHOCOLATE CHIP Add 1 teaspoon mint extract. Toward the end of churning, toss in ¾ cup chocolate chips.

SUGAR-FREE VANILLA OR CHOCOLATE BANANA Omit the sugar and use in its place 1 to 1½ cups mashed, ripe bananas. Reduce the water by ½ cup and add 1 tablespoon good-quality vanilla extract. For chocolate, add ½ cup cocoa powder.

luscious low-fat vanilla oat gelato

Luscious isn't a word that usually describes oil-free foods. But luscious is the best way to describe this creamy frozen dessert. What's the secret? Oats. Technically, it's frozen oatmeal. I know. That doesn't make you salivate. But taste this and you will believe. It's the next best thing to artisan vegan cheese. And if you want to leave the sugar out, you can just sweeten to taste with stevia, erythritol, or dates.

4 cups nondairy milk

½ cup cashews

¼ cup rolled oats

⅔ cup organic sugar (or stevia to taste)

4 vanilla beans, split lengthwise

Place 2 cups of the milk and the cashews in a blender and puree until smooth. Then pour it into a large (2-quart) saucepan over medium heat along with the remaining 2 cups milk, oats, sugar, and vanilla beans. Bring to a boil, turn down the heat, and simmer for about 15 minutes, until the mixture has thickened slightly and the oats are very soft. You should have about 4 cups. Allow it to cool to room temperature, then pour it into a blender and process until smooth and creamy. Transfer to a covered container and put it in the refrigerator until cold.

Pour the mixture into an ice cream maker and churn according to the manufacturer's instructions. Don't be put off when the ice cream comes out of the machine with a bit of a stretchy or gummy texture—after freezing for a few hours, this will turn to creaminess. Keep some gelato on hand in your freezer for 2 to 3 months so you can have a scoop when the urge hits!

MAKES ABOUT 4 CUPS

CUSTOMIZE YOUR GELATO

Try your own flavor combinations! Add some finely ground espresso for coffee gelato (or add a dash of rum for coffee rum gelato!), pour in a ribbon of freshly made Not-Tella Chocolate Hazelnut Spread (page 42), or sweeten with maple syrup and add cinnamon for Maple Cinnamon Gelato! The combinations are endless, and you'll feel good knowing you're putting healthy ingredients into your body while your palate thinks you're indulging.

luscious low-fat chocolate oat gelato

Rich, creamy, and almost sin-free.

3 cups nondairy milk

¼ cup rolled oats, regular or instant

⅓ cup organic sugar, maple syrup,
or coconut sugar

¼ cup cocoa powder

2 ounces dark or semisweet chocolate

1 tablespoon vanilla extract

Combine the milk, oats, and sweetener in a 2-quart saucepan over medium heat. Bring to a boil, turn down the heat to low, and simmer for about 15 minutes, until the mixture is somewhat thick and the oats are very soft. Add the cocoa powder, dark chocolate, and vanilla. Stir until completely smooth and creamy and no lumps of cocoa or chunks of dark chocolate remain. Let it cool briefly, then pour it into a blender and process until smooth and creamy (remove the cap from the lid to allow steam to escape and cover the hole with a kitchen towel while blending). Then transfer to the refrigerator until it is very cold.

Pour the mixture into an ice cream maker and churn according to the manufacturer's instructions. Store in your freezer for 2 to 3 months.

MAKES ABOUT 4 CUPS

VARIATION

LUSCIOUS LOW-FAT PUMPKIN SPICE OAT GELATO Combine 3 cups milk, ¼ cup rolled oats, ¾ cup maple syrup, 1 cup canned pumpkin, and 2 teaspoons pumpkin pie spice, then cook, puree, chill, and churn in an ice cream maker as instructed above.

fresh fruit sorbet

This is a recipe for a fruit-only sorbet with no sugar added. But don't think it'll be boring. The variations are only as limited as your imagination, and you can create exciting flavor combinations that you can feel good about eating. Strawberry Basil Sorbet, anyone? How about Pineapple Mint Lime? Or Mango Coconut? You can have it all, and know you're eating only fruit!

---

2 ripe bananas

3 cups frozen fruit, such as mango, pineapple, strawberries, raspberries, blueberries, young coconut, or any combination

½ cup orange juice or other fruit juice

Fresh mint leaves, lemon or lime zest, lavender flowers, fresh basil, citrus oils, or extracts, for flavor (optional)

In a blender, combine all of the fruit and juice and puree until smooth. Add the desired flavorings. Transfer to an ice cream maker and process according to the manufacturer's instructions. Because the mixture will already be very cold coming out of the blender, you won't need to process it very long. Keep the sorbet in a closed container in the freezer for 2 to 3 months.

MAKES ABOUT 4 CUPS

slice and bake chocolate chip cookies

There was a time in my life when my husband would request chocolate chip cookies on a weekly basis. Of course, I didn't like baking a whole batch every week for several reasons. First of all, it was a hassle to bake a batch from scratch at ten o'clock on Thursday night when hubby got a sudden craving. I also didn't want several dozen cookies lying around the house tempting me all week, nor did I want them to go stale.

Slice and bake cookies to the rescue! These are really tasty, and you can have the dough log in your fridge ready for fresh cookiedom whenever you want. You can bake just one, two, three, or as many cookies as you want and then tuck the dough log in the fridge for the next time. These are also enhanced by a bit of coffee and notes of toffee from the coconut sugar, creating an exemplary chocolate chip cookie.

---

1 cup Glorious Butterless Butter (page 58), at room temperature

1 cup coconut sugar

⅓ cup organic sugar

3 tablespoons nondairy yogurt

1 teaspoon vanilla extract

2½ cups all-purpose flour

1 tablespoon finely ground coffee

1 teaspoon baking soda

1¼ cups chocolate chips

In a large bowl, cream the butter with both sugars, using an electric mixer or a wooden spoon. Mix in the nondairy yogurt and vanilla. In a large bowl, sift together the flour with the coffee and baking soda, then mix into the butter mixture. Stir in the chocolate chips.

You can bake them right away (if you must!), or you can roll them into two logs about 10 inches long to store and bake later. Wrap the logs well in plastic wrap and put them in a ziplock bag. You can keep them in the refrigerator for 4 to 5 weeks, and slice off one, two, three, or as many cookies as you want to bake off whenever the urge strikes. To bake, preheat the oven to 350°F and line a baking sheet with parchment paper. If your dough is fresh (before rolling into logs), drop by spoonfuls onto the baking sheet. If they are logs, slice about ⅓ inch thick. Bake for 8 to 10 minutes, until golden brown.

MAKES ABOUT 40 COOKIES

florentine cookies

I hadn't had Florentines since I'd gone vegan in my twenties, and I had basically forgotten about their existence. Then a few years ago, I went to Belgium. There, wandering in and out of chocolate shops, I encountered platters piled high with these elegant waferlike cookies full of almonds and glazed with chocolate. I was truly tempted. When I got home, I got to work right away creating a vegan version. I piled them high on a platter at a holiday party and let everyone else rediscover them, too.

2 cups sliced almonds

¼ cup all-purpose flour, oat flour (see sidebar, page 162), or store-bought gluten-free flour

Zest of 1 orange

Pinch of salt

½ cup organic sugar

½ cup maple syrup

3 ounces Glorious Butterless Butter (page 58)

3 tablespoons Cashew Cream (page 56)

1 teaspoon Homemade Vanilla Extract (page 203)

6 ounces dark chocolate, melted (see sidebar, page 197)

Preheat the oven to 350°F. Line two baking sheets with parchment paper. In a large bowl, break up the almond slices a little by hand. Mix with the flour, zest, and salt. In a medium saucepan over medium-low heat, combine the sugar, syrup, butter, cashew cream, and vanilla. Bring to a boil, and then continue to boil for about 2 minutes. Pour this over the almond-flour mixture and mix well with a wooden spoon. If you don't care what shape they are, you can bake them right away: drop by teaspoons, at least 3 inches apart, onto the baking sheets—they spread a lot, and not giving them adequate space will result in one giant wafer. To make them perfectly round, let the mixture cool for at least 30 minutes, then roll them into little balls. Bake for 8 to 10 minutes, until golden brown. Let them cool completely on the pan before attempting to remove, or they will break. You can dip one end in melted chocolate, then set on racks to dry, or drizzle the whole thing in a zigzag fashion with melted chocolate—the choice is up to you. Store the Florentines in an airtight container for up to 1 week, preferably in the refrigerator. To keep them longer, keep them in the freezer for up to 2 or 3 months.

MAKES ABOUT 5 DOZEN COOKIES

chocolate almond polenta puffs

We have a little cabin tucked away in the mountains far from pretty much everything. There's no Internet, television, or cell phone reception, and that quiet takes me to a calm, happy place where the simplest things are joyful. One winter, when the weather was bad and we had little to do, I decided we needed a sweet treat. I dug around the cabinets to see what ingredients I could find. There was a little bit of this and a little bit of that, and I figured a passable cookie could be made. Instead, the cookies exploded in our mouths with rich, chocolaty flavor and an unexpected, delicate crunch from the polenta. Not only are they delicious, but they also never fail to take me back to that wonderful cold, rainy, winter day in our little cabin.

1 cup lightly packed almond meal

1 cup whole wheat pastry flour

½ cup dry polenta (coarse cornmeal)

1 teaspoon baking powder

1 teaspoon instant coffee (optional)

½ cup canola oil

½ cup Sucanat or rapadura (evaporated cane juice) or organic sugar

5 ounces semisweet or dark chocolate, melted (see sidebar, page 197)

1 teaspoon vanilla extract

Preheat the oven to 350°F. Line two baking sheets with parchment paper. Combine the almond meal, flour, polenta, and baking powder in a bowl and mix well with a whisk. For a mocha flavor, add instant coffee to the dry ingredients. Add the oil and mix well; it will look crumbly and wet. Add the evaporated cane juice and mix to incorporate, then mix in the chocolate and vanilla and combine to form a sticky, dark dough.

With your hands, form forty balls. Keep washing your hands so the balls don't stick (your hands can be wet while you roll). Place them on the baking sheets 2 inches apart. Bake for about 10 minutes. They will feel slightly hard on top when they are ready. While warm, they are crumbly and will easily fall apart, so let them cool a bit before popping one in your mouth. These cookies should be kept in an airtight container at room temperature, preferably for no longer than a week or so.

MAKES ABOUT 30 COOKIES

acknowledgments

What fun I had writing this book! It all started with my wonderful agent, Sally Ekus, who ever so patiently guided me through the labyrinth of the manuscript proposal process. What an ear she has! I was certain she would banish me to her blacklist of clients who take up her time and produce little, but she had all the time in the world for me. I thank you wholeheartedly, Sally!

Sally helped me land at Ten Speed Press, a publisher I had admired since I first saw *White Trash Cooking* back in the 1980s. What I'd do to get a contract with them, I thought then! And now, thirty years later, I'm thrilled to be working with them. I thank you, Ten Speed, and my editor, Lisa Regul, for believing in me!

Then there was the whole process of conceiving of handcrafted staples and minimizing waste at every corner. I'd awake each day with new ideas and imagine turning this book into several volumes. Of course, I'd have to build a few new shelves in my pantry. And that's exactly what one of my testers did. One day, Heather Legrand showed up with tools and shelving and doubled my usable pantry space.

From the beginning, there were testers in remote places who joyfully volunteered to see if my recipes held true. Kelly Cavalier led the pack, testing anything and everything I threw at her. Matthew Russell was a close second, as were my friends and former students Laura Verduzco and Alonia Rose. Hana Low, Nichole Kraft, Debbie Knight, Christina Martin, Becky Duncan, and Adam Caswell also tested for me, and I extend my gratitude to all of you. Sheila Tajima helped me in the kitchen with other projects and provided me with a sounding board for my frustrations.

But closer to home, a band of amazing women began to assemble every Wednesday at my house to test my recipes, often in rudimentary stages of development. What began as work turned into play. We cooked, we burned things, we spilled things, and we laughed. We formed such a tight bond and friendship that when the final week came, when there were no more things to test, we were very sad. Our Wednesdays would be no more—or at least not until my next book. Until then, I can't say enough to show my appreciation for all of you—Camala Casco, Linda Postenreider, Heather Legrand, LaVonne Vashon, and Penelope Low—you have added so much to my life the past few months! Also, thanks to a couple of folks who joined us once or twice— Matt Smith, Alicia Robb, and Penelope's mom, Hazel.

Lastly, I can't forget my family, who patiently accepted whatever was left over from testing that day as their evening meal. Sometimes, it would be an odd combination, like ketchup, bread, and meringues, with a little salad thrown in. I think they'll be glad that I can again refocus on real meals.

index

Copyright © 2015 by Miyoko Schinner
Photographs copyright © 2015 by Eva Kolenko

Published in the United States by Ten Speed Press,
an imprint of the Crown Publishing Group, a division
of Random House LLC, a Penguin Random House
Company, New York.
www.crownpublishing.com
www.tenspeed.com

Ten Speed Press and the Ten Speed Press colophon
are registered trademarks of Random House LLC.

Library of Congress Cataloging-in-Publication Data
Schinner, Miyoko Nishimoto, 1957–
  The homemade vegan pantry : the art of making
your own staples / Miyoko Schinner.
     pages cm
1. Vegan cooking. 2. Meat substitutes. 3. Ingredient
substitutions (Cooking) 4. Groceries. I. Title.
 TX837.S322 2015
 641.5'636—dc23
                                    2014036764

Hardcover ISBN: 978-1-60774-677-5
eBook ISBN: 978-1-60774-678-2

Printed in China

Design by Ashley Lima
Food styling by Lillian Kang
Prop styling by Glenn Jenkins

10 9 8 7 6 5 4 3 2 1

First Edition